MASTER

YOUR

MEMORY

MASTER
YOUR
MEMORY

Learn Simple, Effective Techniques to
Remember Anything in any Course or Meeting

Instantly Remember Names and Faces

Never Lose Your Eyeglasses or Keys Again!

From America's Top Expert
on Study Skills

Ron Fry

CAREER
PRESS
Pompton Plains, N.J.

MASTER YOUR MEMORY
TYPESET BY KARA KUMPEL
Cover design by Jon Friedman
Printed in the U.S.A.

To order this title, please call toll-free 1-800-CAREER-1 (NJ and Canada: 201-848-0310) to order using VISA or MasterCard, or for further information on books from Career Press.

CAREER
PRESS

The Career Press, Inc.
12 Parish Drive
Wayne, NJ 07470
www.careerpress.com

Library of Congress Cataloging-in-Publication Data
CIP Data Available Upon Request.

Contents

Introduction

It's All in Your Mind

A man should keep his little brain attic stocked with all the furniture that he's likely to use, and the rest he can put away in the lumber-room of his library, where he can get it if he wants it.
—Sir Arthur Conan Doyle

You misplace your glasses (keys, purse) every day.

You just walked out of a test, frustrated and discouraged, because you knew the material, you *really* knew it—you just didn't remember it *then*.

The last time you had to give a sales presentation, you lost your place in your "memorized speech" and froze, unable to continue.

You ran from one room to another like a frenzied cat… then couldn't remember why.

In other words, you are just like virtually every person on the planet who didn't learn the methods, techniques, and systems that will make remembering almost anything for as long as you want (or need) to so much easier.

I can relate to every one of these examples (and many more!). Before anyone had GPS, navigators, or cell phones—in other words, the Dark Ages—I met a girl at a concert. She gave me her address just in case I got lost trying to follow her home. I did get lost, and I did forget the address, and I was sorry!

I have bombed tests on subjects I knew backward and forward. I have spent hours looking for keys, glasses, phones, and "that little piece of paper I need to remember to bring to work." And when I was a salesperson selling magazine ad space, I confidently answered a question about my publication's circulation with a resounding "Uhhhhhh."

We all have average memories

Virtually all of us start with the same "basic" memory abilities, no more, no less. Some of us are a little better in some areas than others—I have a gift for numbers, remember far too much trivia, and have become pretty adept at remembering cards while playing bridge or poker. But if I didn't actually work at it, I would probably forget my best friend's name. I am completely lost in social situations, and I would have great difficulty memorizing a poem, song, or script word-for-word. And I still manage to lose my glasses occasionally.

But when I *choose* to—and we will soon see how important that *interest* is—and apply some of the memory techniques you're going to learn in this book, I can virtually eliminate my weakest areas and strengthen my strongest.

What does an "average" memory look like? If I tested you on how many digits, names, faces, or random words you could memorize in a minute (and I will in Chapter 2), many of you would remember 7 to 10 of each. Not usually less, not many more. Again, some of you will be a little better at one kind of task than another. But without some training, without learning ways to *improve your memory,* even remembering a 10-item grocery list may be a chore.

Astounding feats of memory athletes

Memory "athletes" participate in local, national, or World Memory Championships, and they can do some astounding feats.

In 2015, the *Guinness Book of World Records* announced that Rajveer Meena had memorized the value of *pi* to 70,000 places. (*Guinness* doesn't recognize Akira Haraguchi's claim that he recited *pi* to 100,000 places in 2006.)

In 2016, Alex Mullen, a second-year medical student at the University of Mississippi, became the first American to win the World Memory Championships. Among other accomplishments, he memorized a single deck of 52 cards in 18.653 seconds, 28 decks (plus four cards) in an hour, 3,029 digits in one hour, and 505 shapes in 15 minutes.

Interestingly, memory training is *task specific*. Chess masters can glance at a board and almost immediately recognize its patterns. Ask them a few hours later to reproduce it and they will. But if the pieces on the board were set up entirely randomly, they will recall it about as well as you would. In other words, not at all!

Memory athletes who can memorize umpteen decks of playing cards in a few minutes wouldn't remember the "random" chess board either. They are average—just like you and me—in any memory test for which *they have not specifically trained.*

Journalist Joshua Foer observed the 2005 USA Memory Championships to write a piece for *Slate* magazine. Intrigued, he decided to try some of the techniques the memory athletes used to see how they would work for him. He not only entered the competition the next year, he won (and chronicled his year-long efforts and the competition in the best-selling *Moonwalking With Einstein*).

But although he had mastered a variety of sophisticated memory techniques, he sometimes found their usefulness in the "real" world less than overwhelming: "Even once I'd reached the point where I could squirrel away more than 30 digits per minute in memory palaces, I still only sporadically used the techniques to memorize the phone numbers of people I actually wanted to call. Occasionally I'd memorize shopping lists, directions, to-do lists, but only in the rare circumstances when there wasn't a pen available to jot them down. It's not that the techniques didn't work. I am walking proof that they do. It's that it is so hard to find occasions to use them in the real world in which paper, computers, cell phones, and post-its can handle the tasks of remembering for me."

Can it really be true that unless we practice memory techniques we are all just, well, average? What about London cabbies, who have to pass what some have called the toughest test in the world—the "Knowledge"—which requires them to memorize 320 basic routes, 25,000 streets, and 30,000 point of interest (from hotels, restaurants, and schools to police stations, landmarks, and tourist attractions)? Do they have some innate ability attributable to warm beer or a plethora of fish and chips?

No. They invariably use the techniques we are going to discuss in far more detail in the following chapters. As Ed Cooke, a British grand memory master, told Foer: "My memory is quite average. All of us (memory athletes) have average memories."

So how hard do we have to work at this?

It does not take an extraordinary mind to develop an extraordinary memory.

I am pretty sure most of you do not plan on driving a London cab or want to see how fast you can memorize a deck of cards. Most of you face similar if less overwhelming memory tasks: If you are a high school, college, or graduate student, you need to be able to recall important dates in history, authors and their books, chemical formulas and equations, scientific laws, important legal cases, or even every nerve, muscle, and bone in the human body. Teachers need to recall detailed lesson plans; coaches need to remember detailed practice plans.

Salespeople have to remember product specs, competitive information, and details about their customers, especially their names and faces! (And so do non-salespeople, especially if you are on a cruise and still can't remember the names of the three other couples at your dining table. And wouldn't it be nice if you could master the basics of the language of the country you're traveling to?) Numerous professions require occasional speeches or presentations. We all have to remember more of what we read, whether it is a school subject, business report, or just a newspaper or magazine article. And it would be just wonderful if we could find our glasses, keys, and purse—right now—and not forget half the items on our shopping list (or leave the list in the car) every time we head to the store.

I guarantee you can vastly improve all of the above by reading this book.

It is not clear that just "practicing more" (mentally, not physically) will do very much, *unless you are practicing a proven technique.* Even then, you will get better at that *particular* activity (remembering numbers, names and faces, historical dates, or authors and books) but not *all* activities.

You may still forget some things, just not as much and not as often, but you will become significantly better at remembering what you want (or need) to remember when you need to remember it.

Okay, okay, tell me the secret!

There is no single, magical memory technique. There are specific techniques for particular situations—remembering facts, memorizing numbers, recalling lists, dealing with scientific equations, and many more—and I will show you all of them. But then you get to choose those techniques or systems that best work for *you*.

Many demonstrations of awe-inspiring memory feats may be seen as just glorified party tricks—impressive, but not particularly useful. Give someone a deck of cards, let him look at them for a few minutes, and he will read them back to you in order. Or introduce him to 100 people and a couple of hours later he will rattle off their names (and birthdays and kids' names) without missing a beat. Ex-NBA player (and memory expert) Jerry Lucas memorized the first *30,000* names and phone numbers in the Manhattan telephone directory to promote his book.

Really? Do *you* need to do that?

I didn't think so.

Many of the other memory books you will find at your local bookstore (or on Amazon) are written by authors touting their national or international memory championship credentials. Some of the techniques covered in their books are pertinent only to specific tests at said championships, such as memorizing binary numbers (using only zeros and ones), shapes, magazine pages, spoken numbers, or single or multiple decks of cards. I should also note that many of these books are relatively old, predating smartphones, and spend a chapter or more on things like memorizing your weekly appointments or being able to tell someone the day of the week for any date in history. Smartphones, of course, also make it easy to create shopping lists or to-do lists, or store phone, credit card, identification, and other important numbers, but I have still included the many techniques that will make it easy to remember any of these…for when you can't find your phone.

With the exception of a brief section of Chapter 10, in which I discuss memorizing cards, I see no particular reason to burden you with things you will never utilize. This does not mean that many of the techniques these experts use aren't included here. They are. But the examples I include and the emphasis on their use is all more practical, more every day, and will hopefully appeal to the vast majority of you.

I am not a memory athlete. I have never entered any such championship, nor do I expect to. I did, however, write a book called *How to Study* some three decades ago. Now in its eighth edition, it has helped millions of students (and others) hone basic study skills, get organized, manage their time, do better on tests, and much more. And although one chapter is devoted to improving your memory, it was clearly not sufficient for the many readers or seminar participants who have asked me for years to do a book encompassing the widest possible variety of memory techniques and systems.

This is that book.

For those of you who want to impress your friends by reciting *pi* to 100 places or 50 random words or every Civil War battle ever fought, you will certainly learn the techniques to do so and can then proceed to awe your friends. And if you are entranced by the idea of entering a memory championship, go for it!

Many of you can immediately improve your memories with a single change of habit: *Write more things down.* As Samuel Johnson noted, "Knowledge is of two kinds: we know a subject ourselves, or we know where we can find information upon it." And he said that, of course, long before Google was around.

Here's the plan

- In Chapter 1, we will talk briefly about the brain and the concept of memory—how it works and why it sometimes doesn't.

- In order to give you a realistic starting point, I have included a series of quizzes in Chapter 2. You do not have to score them or grade yourself, but they will help you gauge your progress when you take a similar series of quizzes at the end of the book.

- Basic memory techniques—acronyms and acrostics, sound-alikes, associations, the link and story systems—are introduced in Chapter 3.

❦ Chapter 4 includes a variety of alphabet systems and my favorite, the Loci ("Places") or Roman House system. After reading these two chapters, and practicing their techniques, you will easily be able to recall a list of 20, 30, even 50 items, such as grocery lists, football plays, or the Periodic Table of the Elements.

❦ By the end of Chapter 5, you will be an expert at recognizing and recalling the names and faces of as many people as you need to, whether at a social party or business function.

❦ Chapter 6 will help you learn how to remember more of what you read no matter how *fast* you read.

❦ Chapter 7 will help you learn how to decipher, spell, and remember unfamiliar English words and quickly master basic vocabulary in many foreign languages.

❦ Chapters 8 and 9 introduce a variety of systems to remember numbers, which will also make recalling equations, formulas, and even license plates easier.

❦ Chapter 10 shows some of the ways to utilize the learned techniques for giving speeches and presentations, memorizing directions and complex passwords, or recalling historical dates. I have also included brief sections on memorizing cards and creating your own "mental calendar."

❦ Chapter 11 is specifically for students or anyone facing any kind of test. You'll learn how to make sure that a fact on "the tip of your tongue" actually makes it to "the front of your brain."

💡 Finally, you get to take another series of quizzes in Chapter 12. After comparing your results at the end of the book, I am confident you will be pleasantly surprised by how much stronger you have made your memory.

Chapter 1

How We Remember and Why We Forget

All thought is a feat of association: having what's in front of you bring up something in your mind that you almost didn't know you knew.
—Robert Frost

The essence of memory is the ability to get in touch with a fact or sensation *as if it just happened.* Developing a skilled or practiced memory is to keep facts, formulas, experiences, numbers, names, and faces at your disposal so you can recall them whenever you need or want to.

Why do so many of us forget where we put our car keys, eyeglasses, or cell phones? Because putting these objects down is the most ordinary of occurrences, part and parcel of the most humdrum aspects of our lives. (According to *Readers Digest*, the average adult spends *16 hours a year* searching for misplaced keys.) We have trouble remembering anything to which we are simply not paying attention. We won't remember a phone number spoken to us if we are already picturing our first date with the person.

You can't transform anything—a date, face, name, or fact—into something memorable without at least a modicum of concentration. I could make the case that an awful lot of what we claim to have "forgotten" we simply never knew in the first place; *we never paid attention to it.* That explains the perennially misplaced glasses, keys, and purses and the hollow-eyed walk around the parking lot trying to remember where we left our car. What we have labeled "absentmindedness" is, in many ways, just a *function of inattention.*

Our brains are still mysterious

As I sat down to write this chapter, there was a serendipitous scientific paper that announced, according to the *New York Times*, a "spectacular new map of the brain, detailing nearly 100 previously unknown regions." Since the "known" regions numbered only 83, that would indicate to me how very little we actually know about our brains. Scientists noted that it may take decades to actually uncover each region's functions.

We know so little about our own brains so it should come as little surprise that we know even less about "memory."

Others have used similes and metaphors to explain it: The brain is like a muscle. Exercising it makes it stronger. Memory is like the ROM and RAM of a computer or a big filing cabinet or a large library with endless rows of "memory shelves." Well…no.

As far as we know, there is no single area of the brain—no structure—that houses "memory," nor any group of regions or areas in which different categories of memory are stored. Indeed, the same memory—or different aspects of it—may exist in many areas of the brain, perhaps in different forms. It has been hypothesized that a memory you want to retrieve may have to be "reassembled" from its various pieces, which may help explain why at different times or in different circumstances we actually "remember" things differently, too.

How does memory actually work? How and why do we remember some things and forget others? *Are* they forgotten or just "misplaced"?

Short- and long-term memory

Let's talk about what we *do* know. There are two primary kinds of memory: short-term and long-term. When we talk about "improving our memory" we are really talking about the latter.

Short-term memory has both a limited capacity and a limited duration. Like a Microsoft Word notepad, what's there stays for a little while and then disappears (or, more likely, is simply overwritten). It is remarkably easy to disrupt—we have all gotten up and gone into the next room, then forgotten why. If we have paid attention at all, retrieval is not really a problem; there isn't that much data there to retrieve. It is merely a way station. At many points during our day, we make the decision of which parts of it to "transfer" to long-term memory and which to discard.

Long-term memory is that vast storage depot (but don't think of it as a physical "place") with, according to some scientists, a limitless (or at least darned big) capacity. A February 2016 article in *Scientific American* declared that our brains have a capacity of 2.5 petabytes (that's 2,500,000,000,000,000), the rough equivalent of 20 million four-drawer file cabinets, or half a *trillion* pages of text. As I said, maybe not limitless, but darned big!

Retention is the process by which we store all those bits and bytes of facts, figures, names, faces, experiences, and so much more in long-term memory. Subject to other actions of the mind, what is retained can be recalled when needed. If you think something is important, you will retain it more easily. So convincing yourself that you *must* retain (and recall) something increases your chances of adding it to your storehouse—your long-term memory bank.

Recall is the process by which we are able to *retrieve* those things that we have retained. Recall is subject to strengthening through the process of repetition. The dynamics of our ability to recall are affected by several factors:

- ✓ We most easily recall those things that are of interest to us.
- ✓ Be selective in determining how much you need to recall. All information is not of equal

importance; focus your attention on being able to recall the most *important* pieces of information.

✓ Associating new information with what you already know will make it easier to recall.

✓ Repeat, either aloud or in your mind, what you want to remember. Find new ways to say those things that you want to recall.

✓ Use the new data you have managed to recall in a meaningful way. It will help you recall it the next time.

Recognition is the ability to see new material and recognize it for what it is and what it means. Familiarity is the key aspect of recognition. You will feel that you have "met" this information before, associate it with other data or circumstances, and then recall the framework in which it logically fits.

Memories may well be available—you *know* you know something; it is right there on the "tip of your tongue"—but not easily retrievable. We have all remembered *part* of what we need to know—a face but not a name, a first name but not a last, a historical date but not the person or event associated with it—and struggled to remember the rest. I have frequently been stumped by a crossword puzzle, put it down, returned to it hours later, and immediately recalled what eluded me before.

Failure to recognize someone or something may be a problem with *context*. We often associate particular people with the places we know them from. Have you ever been unable to "place" the "familiar" face of a woman picking up her kids from school, only to later realize it was the barista who has been making your coffee every morning—for months? Because you associated her exclusively with one place, you had difficulty recognizing her in another.

Make mine memorable

What do all "memorable" names, dates, places, and events have in common? The fact that they are *different*. What makes something memorable is how much it differs from our normal experiences (its *extra*ordinariness), which helps our brain distinguish between what we specifically want to remember from the vast, distracting wasteland of similar or competing information we see and hear every day.

So how can some people so easily recite the names, symbols, and atomic weights of the elements of the periodic table—while they're playing (and winning) Trivial Pursuit? Because this information has gotten "tagged" or "coded" in some way. For some people, myriad bits of data are almost automatically tagged so that they can be quite easily and handily stored and retrieved. But if most of us are to have exceptional memories, we must make a special effort and learn the techniques that simplify such "tagging."

Three kinds of memory

The three kinds of memory are visual, verbal, and kinesthetic, *each* of which can be strong or weak, and only the first two of which are associated with your *brain*. This is, of course, a gross simplification of what we term "memory." Surveys have found more than a hundred different memory tasks in everyday life that can cause people problems, each of which requires a different strategy. (Sorry to break it to you, but just because you've learned an easy way to remember a 100-digit number [see chapters 8 and 9] does *not* guarantee that you won't spend your days looking for those darned glasses.) Some have posited that visual and verbal memories may work very differently and even work at different speeds. Most studies show that visual memory exceeds word memory.

To strengthen our verbal memories, we use rhymes, songs, letter substitutions, and other mnemonic gimmicks. But most people have the easiest time strengthening their *visual* memories, which is why so many memory techniques involve forming "mental pictures." See for yourself: Put together two lists—one of a dozen words, the others of a dozen pictures or photographs. Study each for five minutes. Three days from now, try to replicate both lists. I will bet that you remember far more pictures than words.

In addition to these two kinds of memory with which we are all familiar, there is a third kind: *kinesthetic* memory, or what your *body* remembers. Athletes and dancers certainly don't have to be convinced that their muscles, joints, and tendons seem to have their own memories. Neither does anyone who has ever remembered a phone number by moving his fingers and "remembering" how to dial it.

The next time you have to remember a list, any list, say each item out loud and move some part of your body at the same time. A tap dancer can do the time step and remember her history lecture. A baseball pitcher can associate each movement of his windup with another item of a list he has to memorize. Even random body movements will do. For example, if you have to memorize a list of countries, just associate each one with a specific movement. For Botswana, say it aloud while lifting your right arm. For Zimbabwe, rotate your neck. Bend a knee for Lesotho, and raise your left hand for Burkina Faso. Kick Malawi in the shins and twirl your hair for Mauritius. Touch your right big toe for Kyrgyzstan, your left big toe for Kazakhstan; bend your left pinkie for Tajikistan and your right for Turkmenistan.

When you have to remember this list of countries, just start moving! It may look a little strange—especially if you make your movements a little too exotic or dramatic, but if it works for *you*, who cares? (If you are loath to gyrate in public, just saying something you want to remember *aloud* may help: "I'm turning off the stove," "I parked in section R 15," "I'm placing my glasses on top of the file cabinet.")

And you never know when, like Marcel Proust in *Remembrance of Things Past*, the mere *taste* (or smell, sight, sound, or touch) of something from long ago will conjure up a cascade of "forgotten" impressions: "Undoubtedly what is thus palpitating in the depths of my being must be the image, the visual memory which, being linked to that taste, is trying to follow it into my conscious mind," as he remembered the garden, house, church, town square, streets, and country roads of his childhood, all triggered by the taste of a tea-soaked cookie.

Why we forget

As you think about the elements of developing good memory, you can use them to address why you *forget*. The root of poor memory is usually found in one of these areas:

- We fail to make the material meaningful.
- We fail to grasp what is to be remembered.
- We do not have the desire to remember.
- We fail to associate what we want to remember to something we already know.
- We fail to make our verbal or visual "tags" vivid, unusual, even bizarre or lewd and, therefore, memorable.
- We do not use the knowledge we have gained.

As you will see in the following chapters, your imagination and creativity are the basis for every memory technique you will learn. Randomness must be given structure, the meaningless made meaningful, the easily forgettable made memorable.

Chapter 2

How Good Is Your Memory Right Now?

This chapter contains a series of tests that will help determine your "memory starting line," or what and how much you can remember right now. There is no reason to get anxious; the "score" for each test is only so you can see how you do on the tests in Chapter 12, after learning the many techniques in this book, compared to where you started.

Test 1: Random numbers

Look at the following number for no more than two minutes. Then cover the page (or, better yet, close the book and put it aside) and write down as much of it—in order—as you can.

03995121571143091041251

Test 2: Random words

Study the following list of words for no more than two minutes, then cover the page and reproduce as many words as you can. (Pats on the back for listing them in the correct order.)

Skirt	Beard
Pipe	Cigar
Car	Glass
Shovel	Chair
Umbrella	Stove
Daisy	TV
Rocket	Spoon
Bone	Tiger
Tuba	Magazine
Butter	Sky

Test 3: Less-familiar English words and definitions

The following list contains 15 obscure English words along with their definitions. Study it for three minutes, then take a separate sheet of paper and write down as many of the words and definitions as you can. Their order is not important. Allow yourself no more than an additional three minutes to complete the quiz.

Discalced	Barefoot
Soporific	Sleepy or drowsy
Claque	A group hired to applaud an act or performer
Damson	A small dark blue plum
Pollex	Thumb
Eristic	Pertaining to controversy
Leman	Mistress
Imprest	A loan
Costard	A large, English variety of apple
Valgus	Bow-legged
Thistly	Troublesome
Horripilation	Goosebumps
Edentulous	Toothless
Tiffin	A light lunch
Lowery	Dark, threatening

Test 4: Foreign words and definitions

Look at the following list of 15 German words along with their English definitions. Study this list for three minutes, then take a separate sheet of paper and write down as many of the words and definitions as you can. Their order is not important. Allow yourself no more than an additional three minutes to complete the quiz.

Esel	Donkey
Rezept	Prescription
Holz	Wood
Nebel	Fog
Teich	Pond
Zahn	Tooth
Dorf	Village
Klavier	Piano
Obst	Fruit
Tuch	Kerchief
Augriff	Attack
Schrei	Scream
Wissen	Knowledge
Geflugel	Poultry
Pilz	Mushroom

Test 5: Names

Give yourself three minutes to memorize the names of the following U.S. president/vice president combinations, then take another three minutes to write down as many as you remember. Order is not important, though the correct pairing is.

Thomas Jefferson/George Clinton

Martin Van Buren/Richard Johnson

Ulysses S. Grant/Skuyler Colfax

Harry Truman/Alben Barkley

James Monroe/Daniel Tompkins

James Polk/George Dallas

Andrew Jackson/John C. Calhoun

Franklin Pierce/William King

James Buchanan/John C. Breckinridge

Grover Cleveland/Thomas Hendricks

Test 6: Historical dates

Give yourself three minutes to memorize the names and dates of the following Civil War battles, then take another three minutes to write down as many as you remember. Order is not important, though pairing is.

May 12, 1863	Battle of Raymond
November 7, 1861	Battle of Belmont
May 25, 1862	Battle of Winchester
September 14, 1862	Battle of South Mountain
July 1, 1863	Battle of Gettysburg
April 12, 1861	Battle of Fort Sumter
June 25, 1862	The 7 Days Battle
March 8, 1862	The Battle of Pea Ridge
October 9, 1861	The Battle of Santa Rosa Island
September 18, 1863	Battle of Chickamauga

Here is another list, this time of the finalists (but not the winner) for the Pulitzer Prize for Drama for five different years. Again, give yourself three minutes to memorize the names of the plays, playwrights, and dates, then take another three minutes to write down as many as you remember. Order is not important, though pairing the correct date with the correct play and playwright is.

2003	*Take Me Out*	Richard Greenberg
	The Goat or Who Is Sylvia?	Edward Albee
1996	*A Fair Country*	Jon Robin Baitz
	Old Wicked Songs	Jon Marans

| 1984 | *Fool for Love* | Sam Shepard |
| | *Painting Churches* | Tina Howe |

| 2014 | *Fun Home* | Lisa Kron, Jeanine Tesori |
| | *The (Curious Case of the) Watson Intelligence* | Madeline George |

| 1987 | *A Walk in the Woods* | Lee Blessing |
| | *Broadway Bound* | Neil Simon |

Test 7: Lists without dates

Look at this list of states and their respective state flowers (no dates!). Again, give yourself three minutes to memorize the combinations, then take another three minutes to write down as many as you remember. Order is not important.

New York	Rose
Vermont	Red clover
Maryland	Black-eyed susan
Louisiana	Magnolia
Kansas	Sunflower
Nevada	Sagebrush
Illinois	Violet
Tennessee	Iris

Wyoming	Indian paintbrush
Arkansas	Apple blossom
Missouri	Hawthorn
Utah	Sego lily

Test 8: Reading

Read the following passage at your normal reading speed, and then answer the questions.

The brain is subdivided into four major areas. From the top down, you'll find: 1) the *cerebral cortex,* which I refer to as the cortex; 2) the *midbrain*, which contains a lot of the switching areas where nerves that pass up from below go to and from the cortex; 3) the *brainstem*, where much of the basic nervous system controls sit (coma occurs when this malfunctions, and death occurs when it is severed); and 4) the *cerebellum,* which sits behind the upper part of the brainstem and has traditionally been thought to regulate coordination of complex movements.

The cerebral cortex is the most newly evolved region of the brain and it is the part that separates humans from all the other mammals, especially the area in the front, appropriately named the *frontal cortex*. This area acts as a bridge between the sensory and motor circuits of the rest of the cortex and the older, deeper structures of the limbic system, which regulate drive and emotion. The frontal cortex is probably where much of our complex and abstract thoughts occur. It is probably where we put today in context with yesterday and tomorrow. When the frontal lobe is damaged, we become either more reactive and hypersexual like wild animals (without the step of logic in between to stop us) or very docile and unconcerned.

Behind the frontal cortex are the sensory and motor regions of the cortex, each divided up to correspond with specific areas on the opposite side of the body. Along the side are two protruding horns of cortex called the *temporal lobes*. Here, much of the processing of sound and verbal information occurs. Inside sits a deeper part of the limbic system called the *hippocampus*. The hippocampus acts like a way-station that coordinates the placement of information as it moves from sensory input to other areas of the brain.

In the back is the *occipital cortex*, where much of the processing of visual information occurs. The remaining areas along the side above the temporal horns form the *parietal cortex*. These areas are thought to be where a lot of cross-connection between the different sensory structures occurs. When the right side of the parietal cortex is damaged, very bizarre perceptions and reactions occur, such as ignoring one side of your body because you think it is a stranger.

The limbic system consists of the hippocampus, the rim of cortex on the inside of the halves around the corpus callosum called the *cingulate cortex*, and two almond-shaped heads near the frontal region, each one called the *amygdala*. This set of structures is the closest thing to what Freud referred to as the id, the seat of emotion and animal drive. It is the older region of the cortex in terms of evolution, and is also involved in memory.

Strange things can happen when the cortex is damaged. (A great book on this subject is *The Man Who Mistook His Wife for a Hat*, by Dr. Oliver Sacks.) I find this particularly fascinating because it means who you are as a person in terms of identity and interaction with other people depends completely on the complex and precise interaction of all these neural areas. It suggests that your identity depends on your neurology and not merely on a spirit living in your body.

1. Which part of the brain processes much of the visual information?
2. What are the temporal lobes?
3. What occurs if the brainstem malfunctions?
4. What is the most newly evolved region of the brain?
5. How many major areas is the brain subdivided into?

Did you do better on some of these tests than others? Are you a whiz with numbers (test 1) but pathetic with remembering dates (test 6)? Can you remember grocery or to-do lists easily (test 2) but fail with names (test 5)?

This will indicate how much improvement you need to successfully recall the material you are currently forgetting. It will also provide a benchmark so that you can see how far you've come when you take similar quizzes in the last chapter.

The emphasis of these tests was not arbitrary. They correspond with the skills you will be learning throughout this book: memorizing chains of information (such as the president/vice president and Pulitzer Prize pairings), developing a sense for numbers, remembering what you read, and getting a better grasp on vocabulary.

Specifically, you will be able to memorize random digits (test 1) far more easily once you have mastered chapters 8 and 9, after which you will realize that remembering the 23-digit number (03995121571143091041251) only requires remembering a single sentence: "Some people don't like to eat worms, but I certainly do." Those chapters will also make you the master of historical dates and events (test 6) and give you a system to memorize any list *in order*.

Chapters 3 and 4 will provide you a wide variety of techniques for memorizing any random word list (test 2) or list pairing (tests 5 and 7). Chapter 5 will also help with those tests and add the ability to match remembered names to appropriate faces.

Chapters 6 and 7 will help you remember more of what you read and increase both your ability to remember less-familiar English words and completely unfamiliar foreign ones (tests 3 and 4).

Let's start learning how to improve our memory.

Chapter 3

Did Richard of York *Really* Give Battle in Vain?

Memories may escape the action of the will, may sleep a long time, but when stirred by the right influence, though that influence be light as a shadow, they flesh into full stature and life with everything in place.

—John Muir

A *mnemonic* (the first "m" is silent) is any technique, system, or trick that helps you remember numbers, names, faces, shopping lists, or anything else, whether your prefer acronyms, phrases, associations, links, stories, rhymes, sound-alikes, or another technique. They work because they impose order on otherwise-unorganized material, and, as we have established, the brain *likes* order and structure.

Mnemonics can be verbal or visual, both of which we will introduce and discuss in this chapter.

Every boy has a FACE

Acronyms are the simplest and most well-known verbal mnemonics. And the simplest of all acronyms create a new word to remember something else. We all probably learned to remember the notes in the spaces of the treble clef in music by thinking of **FACE**. Or remembering **HOMES** to represent the Great Lakes (**H**uron, **O**ntario, **M**ichigan, **E**rie, and **S**uperior).

Many acronyms in our daily life that have nothing to do with memorization have become so ubiquitous that most of us probably don't remember (or never learned) what they stand for in the first place. We probably know that IBM is International Business Machines or that SAT once stood for Scholastic Aptitude Test (but now stands for...nothing). However, we probably talk about going scuba diving without knowing that "SCUBA" stands for **S**elf-**C**ontained **U**nderwater **B**reathing **A**pparatus or play Laser Tag without knowing that "LASER" stands for **L**ight **A**mplification by **S**timulated **E**mission of **R**adiation. Some acronyms are necessary in order to avoid tongue twisting. Would you prefer to go to **IKEA** or **I**ngvar **K**amprad **E**lmtaryd **A**gunnaryd, the actual name of the Swedish furniture company?

Knowing what an acronym means often has a lot to do with context. Business owners know that **EBIDTA** stands for **E**arnings **B**efore **I**nterest **D**epreciation **T**axes and **A**mortization. But acronymfinder.com notes that it also stands for the East Beds Invitation Dart League, the Elephant Butte Irrigation District, and Electron Beam-Induced Deposition, among many others. Some acronyms are unintentionally appropriate, such as CREEP, which stood for Richard Nixon's Committee to Re-Elect the President. Simple acronyms are most prevalent (and helpful) in medicine.

Jones criteria of rheumatic fever can be remembered two ways:

Subcutaneous nodules

Pancarditis

Arthritis

Chorea

Erythema marginatum

or

Chorea

Arthritis

Nodules

Carditis

Erythema marginatum

Rheumatic fever

Horner's syndrome components are PAM (**P**tosis, **A**nhydrosis, and **M**iosis) and Broad Ligament contents can be remembered, helpfully, with BROAD (**B**undle [ovarian neurovascular], **R**ound ligament, **O**varian ligament, **A**rtefacts [vestigial structures], and **D**ucts.

Some people create nonsense acronyms like KFRW or FLORTEX, and then wonder why they don't work. Memory experts have the most trouble remembering lists of three-letter "nonsense words" like NJG, CEU, and SYR, so it follows that "nonsense" acronyms will not work very well, either.

And every Roy a Biv?

The next level of acronym is represented by ROY G. BIV, the name to remind you of the colors of the spectrum in order, from left to right (**R**ed, **O**range, **Y**ellow, **G**reen, **B**lue, **I**ndigo, **V**iolet).

There are a limited number of items that conveniently allow a single word (or, like Roy, a "name") to act as a mnemonic. The vast majority of mnemonics create phrases whose words duplicate the first letters of the list to be remembered. You all learned how to remember the notes that go on the lines of the treble clef (the sidekick to FACE) by learning that **E**very **G**ood **B**oy **D**oes **F**ine (or, in the UK, that he **D**eserves **F**avour). The UK also never heard of Roy G. Biv, but they did learn that **R**ichard **of Y**ork **G**ave **B**attle **i**n **V**ain and prefer to list the Great Lakes from west to east by remembering **S**ome **M**en **H**ate **E**ating **O**nions. (You can remember the Great Lakes by *size* with **S**am's **H**orse **M**ust **E**at **O**ats.)

Do you find that good boy particularly memorable for remembering the treble clef? If not, you can certainly think of another phrase that works for you. How about **E**ven **G**oose **B**erries **D**rive **F**ast? Fans of the King may prefer **E**lvis's **G**uitar **B**aked **D**onuts **F**riday. The *Sesame Street* faithful could remember that **E**rnie **G**ave **B**ert **D**ead **F**rogs (or **D**ates and **F**igs or **D**yed **F**ingers or…).

What if you had to remember the planets in the solar system: Mercury, Venus, Earth, Mars, Jupiter, Saturn, Uranus, Neptune? (Sorry, Pluto.) The possibilities are limited only by your imagination:

My **V**irgin **E**ars **M**ight **J**ust **S**tep **U**pon **N**udists

Many **V**egans **E**at **M**ice, **J**ust **S**how **U**s **N**ighties

My **V**ery **E**ducated **M**other **J**oust**S** **U**sing **N**ikes

I'm sure you can do better. The important thing is to make your new phrase as memorable to you as it can be. It should be unexpected, strange, or weird, and could be violent, sexy, or downright lewd. You just have to remember it (not share it on Facebook).

Remember the line from the end of the quiz: "Some people don't like to eat worms, but I certainly do?" What if you replaced "worms" with "spaghetti," "pasta," "cereal," or "bananas"? Doesn't any such substitution make the resulting picture less memorable? Spaghetti, cereal, et al. are all very *normal* things to eat; their very normality is what makes them less memorable. Ah, but that picture of wriggling worms pouring out of your mouth? Hard to forget—no matter how hard you try!

Likewise, a picture that is vague, is undramatic, and lacks action will also fail. Just picturing a sign saying "worms for sale" or a tin can of worms on a supermarket shelf leaves little lasting impression. Neither will elicit the same strong reaction as an image that reverses our expectations in an exaggerated way.

The hip bone's connected to the, er, uh...

Again, medical students have hundreds of mnemonics they can use to remember anatomy, indications of disease, bodily functions, and much more. You can use the ones that previous generations have created or invent new ones that are particularly memorable to you. Here are some examples, with my own mnemonics. As an exercise, you can use the same lists to develop your versions:

So **L**ong **to P**inky, **T**he **T**humb **C**ame **H**ome (Wrist bones: **S**caphoid, **L**unate, **T**riquetrum, **P**isiform, **T**rapezium, **T**rapezoid, **C**apitate, **H**amate).

The **Z**ither **B**it **M**y **C**ar (Branches of the facial nerve: **T**emporal, **Z**ygomatic, **B**uccal, **M**andibular, **C**ervical).

Hip **F**at **P**atty **T**ied **F**lags **T**o **M**y **P**ig (Leg bones: **H**ip, **F**emur, **P**atella, **T**ibia, **F**ibula, **T**arsals, **M**etatarsals, **P**halanges).

On **O**ld **O**lympus' Towering **T**op **A** **F**inn **A**nd **G**erman **V**iewed **S**ome **H**ogs (Cranial nerves in order: **O**lfactory, **O**ptic, **O**culomotor, **T**rochlear, **T**rigeminal, **A**bducens, **F**acial, **A**uditory [or vestibulocochlear], **G**lossopharyngeal, **V**agus, **S**pinal accessory, **H**ypoglossal).

Some prefer viewing **H**ops to **H**ogs; others drop "spinal" and just use "accessory," in which case they are either "**V**iewing **A** **H**orse" or the Finn and German "**V**ault **A**nd **H**op."

Mnemonic devices like this do not substitute for learning. Unless you are pretty familiar with the glossopharyngeal nerve, the "G" in German is not going to produce it in a flash (in which case you might prefer picturing a soundalike, such as "Glossy" or "Glassy Pharaoh").

Notice that the "memorability" of a phrase like this can be greatly strengthened if it were not just *verbalized* but *visualized*. And isn't it easy to make a picture in your mind of a notable German (your choice!) with a shark fin growing out of his or her head, gazing at a pig pen while standing on a Greek mountain (perhaps with Anthony Quinn as *Zorba the Greek*)? Or vaulting and hopping? Likewise, it shouldn't be hard to picture Patty tying flags to pigs or a zither eating your car (even if you aren't completely sure what a zither is).

What is Della wearing? I'll ask her

Substitute or sound-alike words can make anything memorable, especially if they are also easily pictured. "Cauliflower" is a pretty good stand-in for California (if you are trying to remember 50 states and their capitals, for example). Can you picture your friend George (or Washington or Clooney) with peach juice running down his face? Then you won't forget that Georgia is the Peach state. And what is your friend Della wearing (Delaware)? I'll ask her (Alaska). Others are just as easy: "You there!" (Utah); oregano (Oregon); "Why oh me?" (Wyoming); "How are I?" (Hawaii); and so on.

The more familiar you are with the states, the less need you will have for sound-alikes for every syllable. Won't "Bam" remind you of Alabama (and the 44th president), "where" or "wear" of "Delaware, "ask" of Alaska? Alternatively, just picturing the Empire State Building (or Statue of Liberty), Disney World, and Abraham Lincoln might be all you need to remember New York, Florida, and Illinois.

Once you start becoming adept at picturing sound-alikes, you can easily create a "chain link" to remember items in sequence, whether associating dates with events for history class (or to avoid forgetting a niece's birthday), scientific terms with their meanings, or any other facts that are supposed to go together.

The basis for this method is, as we've previously discussed, memory seems to work best when you associate the unfamiliar with the familiar—*linking* something you need to learn to something you already know. It's the natural evolution from tying a piece of string around your finger or a rubber band on your wrist to remember...*some*thing. Though the "reminder" may not have always reminded us of *what* we were supposed to remember.

Try creating your own chain-link of images to remember the following list of states and their state flowers:

Vermont	Red clover
Maryland	Black-eyed susan
Louisiana	Magnolia
Kansas	Sunflower
Nevada	Sagebrush
Illinois	Violet
Tennessee	Iris
Wyoming	Indian paintbrush
Arkansas	Apple blossom
Missouri	Hawthorn
Utah	Sego lily

Remember: You can use any combination of the mnemonics we've already discussed, though the more visual your connections and the more creative and imaginative your pictures, the easier they will be to remember. Do you have a friend Susan who you can picture with a black eye? Go ahead! How about Iris and Violet (or violent Iris, who perhaps punched your dear friend Susan)? Sure, picture them. Heck, my dentist's name is Dr. Appelbaum. All I have to do is picture him *saw*ing an *ark*.

And kudos to any of you who recognized this list from the previous chapter's quiz. See, your memory is improving already!

Remembering a short list like this—only 20 items remembered with 10 pictures—should not be hard for any of you with a little practice. But as you need to remember longer lists, just "linking" them may become difficult.

Tell me a story

The solution is to combine your pictures into a story. For example, here is a list of the 12 months of the French Revolutionary calendar: Brumaire, Floréal, Frimaire, Fructidor, Germinal, Messidor, Nivôse, Pluviôse, Prairial, Thermidor, Vendémaire, Ventôse. Here's one story I could create to remember this list (and even get pretty close to correctly pronouncing each month):

> There's a big *broom* sweeping through the *air* over a field of *flowers* (Brumaire, Floréal). Suddenly the broom turns into a *fry*ing pan, still flying through the *air* (Frimaire). A pile of *fruit* flies through the *door* (Fructidor), following by my friend *Al* and his *German* shepherd (Germinal).
>
> "You've got a *messy door*," he yells (Messidor) but I just kept making my salad *Niçoise* (Nivôse). "*Pl*ease," I laughed, "no n*oise*" (Pluviôse). Al shoved me to the *prayer rail* (Prairial) to beg for some Lobster *Thermidor* (Thermidor) from the *vend*ing machine that was flying through the *air* (Vendémaire). "Open a *vent* for my *toes!*" (Ventôse), he cried.

Read through my story a couple of times (even though you may have a better one in mind) then put down the book and write out the months. Pretty easy, right?

Here are some other lists for you to try. Remember: Create pictures and stories that are memorable to *you*.

Modes of transportation

Oxen	Rocket
Yacht	Taxi
Van	Zeppelin
Ferry	Bus
Airplane	Glider
Canoe	Auto
Donkey	Palanquin
Kayak	Lorry

Sumerian goddesses and their areas of influence

Ninkasi	alcohol
Ereshkigal	the underworld
Sirtir	sheep
Nammu	sea
Ama	fertility
Ninlil	air
Gula	medicine
Inanna	love
Nidaba	learning
Damkina	Earth
Ningal	reeds
Ashnan	grain
Ninhursag	childbirth

Languages and the country in which they are spoken

Maori	New Zealand
Tepes	Uganda
Adangme	Ghana
Fur	Chad
Livonian	Latvia
Bambara	Mali
Pipil	San Salvador
Adangbe	Togo
Himba	Gabon
Chamorro	Guam
Dalecartian	Sweden
Shena	Zimbabwe
Tok Pisin	Papua New Guinea
Khoekhoe	Namibia

Clearly you don't have to *understand* what you are trying to memorize or even the correct way to pronounce the obscure elements of a list (though correct spelling and, in some stories you will create, the order of items will be important).

The reason is that you use so much more of your brain when you employ techniques like this. Reciting a list of facts over and over to yourself uses only three of your faculties as you try to establish a memory trail: sight (as you read them from the page), speech, and hearing. Constructing a *visual* story like the one we just did also activates your imagination, perhaps your mind's most powerful asset.

Time yourself. When you can construct a series of pictures to remember lists like these—and remember them for a while, not just one day—all in less than five minutes, you are well on your way to mastering this powerful memory technique. Do not expect to reach this point in a day or even a week; the more unusual, unfamiliar, and longer the list, the longer it will initially take you to create a memorable story.

This method is particularly useful for lists that are in no logical order (world capitals, ancient kings, gods and goddesses, languages, and so on) but on which your story *imposes* structure. It is also helpful when working with lists of items already associated to each other, like presidents and vice presidents, authors and books, the Ten Commandments, amendments to the U.S. Constitution, parts of the Bible, directors and their films, and many others.

Here's a summary of how to make any chain-link or story more memorable:

- To the extent possible, make the chain-link scenarios you construct highly *unusual*. If you are linking "fork" to "cereal," better to have a cereal box eating with the fork than just substituting a fork for the spoon in a bowl of cereal.

- Exaggerate your images: A boot as big as Mother Hubbard's house, a truly Big Apple, a grin that's 3 feet wide. The more outrageous, ridiculous, and funny they are, the more you will remember them. I have gone out of my way to avoid X-rated images or stories, but if your mind is bent in that direction, those images can be *very* memorable.

- ☝ Concrete examples and pictures are easier to remember than abstractions; a baseball bat is easier to picture—and remember—than "athleticism," a light bulb easier than "idea."

- ☝ Don't think of an object just sitting there. Have it *do something* (the crazier the better). A broom is sweeping a dog, a table is using a cat to eat on, a TV set is crying.

- ☝ Conjure up a scenario that elicits an *emotional reaction*: joy, sorrow, physical pain, whatever.

- ☝ Many lessons for preschoolers and those in first and second grades are done with *rhymes*. If it works for them, it should work for you, right? So if you are a punster at heart, feel free to construct any that work for you, no matter how tortured.

- ☝ Get comfortable creating your own acronyms for anything you have to remember.

You're probably thinking that all of this doesn't sound like it will make your life any easier. I know it *seems* like a lot of work to think of sound-alikes, associations, and pictures, and construct crazy scenarios using them. Trust me: If you start applying these tips *routinely*, they will become second nature and make remembering any relatively short list a breeze.

And that is the one drawback I must point out: I personally find that after 10 or 15 items, it gets harder to remember the sometimes-long stories that result. (And it is not very easy to answer a question such as "So what is the fifth item in your list?") In Chapter 4, we will solve that problem by introducing some intermediate methods (alphabet files) and the almost unlimited (and my favorite) Roman House or Loci system, which can probably accommodate everything you need to remember (with enough practice). And in chapters 8 and 9, we'll learn a number of mnemonic systems that will allow you to recall lists in whatever order you need—forward, backward, or sideways.

Chapter 4

As Easy as ABC or a Walk in the Park

There is an easy way to automatically extend the list of words or items you can memorize to 26—as long as you remember your ABCs. Just create a series of words and pictures tied to the English alphabet that you can then pair with the items you need to remember.

Here's a list of pictures you could use, with some (but certainly not all) possible substitutes:

Ape (Ax, Awl, Ace)

Boat (Bee, Bicycle, Beanie, Bear, Box, Beer)

Cigar (Computer, Candle, Car, Club, Sea)

Dodo (Dinosaur, Drum, Diamond, Daisy, Dean, Doe)

Ear (Eye, Eel)

Feet (Foil, Fire, Freighter, Football)

Goose (Grass, Girl, Gag, Golf club, Guitar)

Hive (Heaven, House, Hip, Hell, Ham)

Ivy (Eye, Iron, Igloo)

Jet (Jetty, Jar, Jail)

Kite (Kitty, Knight, Cab, Cub, Kerchief, Kumquat)

Leaf (Loaf, Lemon, Leg, Llama)

Mom (Man, Mace, Modem, Metal)

Nun ([K]not, [K]nee, Nose, Noose)

Oar (Oven, Oxen, Owl)

Pipe (Pope, Pot, Peg, Pie, Peel)

Quill (Queen, Quail)

Rope (River, Racer, Robber, Rose)

Soap (Stop sign, Soup, Stump, Saxophone)

Toe (Tub, Tug, Tattoo, Tornedo, Tea, Tee)

Umbrella (Urn, Uzi)

Vampire (Vine, Vein, Vane, Venus)

Wino (Wheel, Wagon, Witch)

X-ray

Yoyo (Yak, Yolk)

Zebra (Zither, Zoo)

There are no particular rules about how to construct your basic alphabet file. It would probably be easiest, of course, to ensure that your word starts with the pertinent letter of the alphabet—**A**pe, **L**eaf, **S**oup, and so on. But you may make an exception for "Eye" and prefer to use it as a sound-alike for "I" or use "Sea" for "C." Rather than using words that start with the initial letter, some people prefer rhyming, so their alphabet might use "Ham" or "Hem" for "M" and so on. If it works for you, rhyme away.

You just need to make the pictures easiest for *you* to remember. An athlete may find it easier to use Football, Golf club, and Tee, for example, whereas a musician might prefer a Drum, Guitar, and Saxophone.

You may even choose all or most of your words from a single category, like musical instruments, sports, and so on. Foodies can choose meats (Cow, Pig, Veal, Sausage, Pepperoni), fruits (Apple, Date, Fig, Lime, Orange, Tangerine, Kumquat), and Vegetables (Kale, Bean, Eggplant) to pepper their own gastronomical list.

A world traveler I know has an alphabet list consisting entirely of places she has visited, key landmarks, even favorite restaurants and museums. Because these are tied to experiences she will never forget, it is a successful idea.

A friend who loves movies uses his favorite celebrities or their characters for his alphabet file: **A**ce Ventura is A (and Jim Carrey is **J**), **B**eyonce is B, **C**her is C, and so on. He can picture these faces so easily it took him no time at all to create his very personalized file (though neither of us could think of an alternative to **X**avier Cugat and he had to picture Zachary **Q**uinto as a young Mr. Spock to remember him). Being older, I had no trouble remembering Anthony **Q**uinn as **Z**orba the Greek.

What do you do with this newly memorized list? Let's say you had a to-do list of 10 chores: Drop the car off, pick up the cleaning, buy milk and cheese at the supermarket, write a thank-you note to a friend, buy a gift for your niece's birthday, pick up the mail, order a pizza for dinner, return a shirt to the department store for credit, buy bagels at the local deli, and call your mother. You could, of course, organize this to-do list in some logical order (certainly wait to drop off your car until you finish your other errands), but let's just remember it in the suggested order:

> An ape is driving your car with a bear in the passenger seat holding a stack of dirty clothes. Ahead of them looms a bright computer screen showing pictures of milk and cheese held by a dinosaur writing a note and standing on a wriggling eel wrapped in birthday envelopes, which suddenly burst into flames (fire). Up in the sky, a goose is flying with a pizza on its back, wearing a shirt made out of ham. The flames go out, and an igloo made out of bagels appears. Your mother is staring out of the bars (jail) of its sole window.

It took me barely a minute to construct this story. With a little more time, I (or you) could probably edit it to make the images and links more vivid, weird, and, therefore, memorable.

Those of you in the military (or veterans) may find it easier to use the alphabet you learned in the service. From Vietnam on, that alphabet is:

Alpha	November
Bravo	Oscar
Charlie	Papa
Delta	Quebec
Echo	Romeo
Foxtrot	Sierra
Golf	Tango
Hotel	Uniform
India	Victor
Juliett	Whiskey
Kilo	X-Ray
Lima	Yankee
Mike	Zulu

Although some of these words are easily pictured (foxtrot, golf, hotel, and so on), I personally would have trouble using Quebec, alpha, echo, and some others. But perhaps you are more creative than I. If you are an older veteran, you learned a different alphabet, perhaps this one used by Marines during the Korean War:

Able	Nan
Baker	Oboe
Charlie	Queen
Dog	Roger
Easy	Sugar
Fox	Tare
George	Uncle
How	Victor
Item	William
Jig	X-Ray
King	Yoke
Love	Zebra
Mike	

The more comfortable you are with the alphabet system you have devised (and the more memorable you have made the images), the easier it will be for you to remember any list up to 26 items.

Let's take a walk

The next system is more than 2,500 years old, making it the oldest memory technique of all. It is called the Roman House or Loci (meaning "Place") System. It was what Cicero and his fellow orators used to memorize speeches, and it was more recently popularized by Benedict

Cumberbatch's Sherlock Holmes, who used hundreds of rooms in his "Memory Palace" to store information.

Let me explain this system by citing an example of how I use it. I have 12 "loci" leading from the top of my driveway to the front door of my house. On the left is a post with a light fixture on top (1), with another on the right (2). As I walk down my driveway, there is a mailbox on the left (3) and a lamppost on the right (4). I have reached my front walk, which has three flower pots—one on the left (5), then one on the right (6), and a third on the left (7). As I reach my front steps, there are two more raised posts with lights—one on the right (8), the other on the left (9). Continuing up the stairs I reach the final ledge, which, again, has two large flower pots—right (10) and left (11). My front door is my 12th loci.

Now, I don't have to do *anything* to remember that walk. I make it multiple times a day, so to remember any 12 items (or steps, or thoughts, or chores, and so on) all I have to do is associate what I am trying to remember (the new) with what I already know (my front walk). Grocery list? Bread is sitting on my left post, eggs are dripping down the second. Batteries are spilling out of my mailbox and a chicken is swinging from the lamppost. Lettuce is growing out of the first flower pot, milk exploding from the second, and a coffee pot percolating in the third.

It takes virtually no time to cement such pictures in my mind. It is so easy I don't even bother to make a written grocery list anymore, which I used to forget (at home or in the car) anyway.

What if I have to remember more than 12 items? Well, there are rooms in my house and they all have furniture or fixtures. I can easily find pictures, faucets, appliances, chairs, tables, sofas, beds, and baths in which to "place" additional items. I have never had to utilize more than a handful for any important list.

And I can easily reuse my front-walk loci for multiple lists. My first list, with my steps alternating left to right, might be for groceries. My second, alternating *right to left*, could help me remember my to-do list. For a third list, I could use the same left-to-right walk *in the rain* or just take the same walk backward—starting at my front door and heading out to the street.

No matter how small your own house or apartment, I am sure you can find dozens of places on which you can "hang" the new items you have to remember. And you certainly aren't limited to using your home. Have you been playing golf on the same course for some time? Even if you have a terrible memory for landmarks you see every day, you can use 18 tees and 18 holes (see the signs, see the flags) to remember 36 items.

Do you walk regularly along a familiar route? Use the buildings and objects you pass to create a new room in your memory palace (or an entirely new palace). Whatever location you are intimately familiar with—the rooms of your home, your town, your garden, your office, golf course, or gym—can be the basis for your own series of loci stored in your personal memory palace(s).

Think of each new list, set of facts, formulas, dates, names, product details, or presentations you have to remember as a separate room in your ever-expanding memory palace. Some of the rooms will be reused often—you really don't have to remember last month's grocery list, do you? Others will remain unchanged for as long as you need them—like until the final exam or sales call or speech is over. The size of your mansion is limited only by your imagination, *not* by your memory.

The Alphabet System may work for you to remember simple lists like grocery items or errands. But many things we have to remember are *paired*—names and faces, dates and events, words and definitions, and so on. I think the Loci System is far easier to use when you have to already create *two* pictures (for each pair) or, at least, an interaction between *two* objects, without having to also tie it to an Ape or Bee or Zebra. The loci should be so firmly cemented in your mind that they require no thought whatsoever to use.

I also think this system offers one huge advantage over the link or story systems: You may forget one item you placed in your room or on your walk, but that won't affect your memory of the others. When you have linked items together, even in a story, forgetting one may well affect your ability to remember any of the other items linked to it.

One last tip: Create a special room in your memory palace that acts like your Microsoft notepad, the place you can "jot down" the random thoughts that occur at the most inopportune times—while you're driving, playing a sport, in a meeting, in class, or going to sleep. You may visit it often and each time you do, you will strengthen the associations that will help you remember to go to the cleaners, write a thank-you note, return that book, and so on.

Here are two more lists for you to memorize using whatever technique(s) you prefer:

Types of Birds

Pacific loon	Gadwall
Eared grebe	Sora
Short-tailed shearwater	Whimbrel
White ibis	Mourning dove
Wood stork	Sky lark
Snow goose	Oliva sparrow
	Bobolink

Types of Music

Merengue	Industrial
Mariachi	Reggae
Jungle	Freestyle
Dixieland	Ragtime

Bluegrass

Celtic

Eurodance

Gothic

House

Skiffle

Bhangra

Vallenato

Trance

Tejano

Illbient

Bossa nova

Andean

Dub

Chapter 5

Oh, Hi There, uh, Buddy

You should always be taking pictures, if not with a camera then with your mind. Memories you capture on purpose are always more vivid than the ones you pick up by accident.

—Isaac Marion

During the nearly 50 years that I knew him, my adopted father, Bill Wright, greeted every woman he met the same exact way: "Hello, Gorgeous!" he would shout, opening his arms and awaiting his (always) forthcoming hug. I never heard or saw a single woman object; they invariably beamed. Although he was undoubtedly impervious to any notion of "political correctness," I never knew whether he simply forgot everyone's name or just enjoyed the glowing smile he usually got in return.

Life is becoming difficult for those of you who simply can't remember names (or can't connect them to faces). Calling female friends or colleagues "love," "honey," "dear," or "sweetheart" is not acceptable. And your male acquaintances undoubtedly assume that when you greet them as "guy," "dude," or "buddy," it is probably because you have completely forgotten who they are.

It's not just embarrassing to forget the name of someone who you met at a party—10 minutes ago. It can be downright career-threatening and bad for business if you consistently forget the names of colleagues, clients, and customers, let alone the managers and executives at your own company.

The good news is that, although you sometimes have to remember someone's full name (and even title), you often only need to remember either a first name *or* a last name. Outside of work-related functions, you will generally be introduced to "Ted and Carol, Brian and Celine, Ed and Candy." Remembering those first names—and being able to connect them with the appropriate faces—is all you need to do.

That may also be true in a work-related setting, though that will depend on your status within the group. If you are one of the top dogs, you will generally greet everyone by first name. As an underling, colleagues will be on a first-name basis but management, executives, big clients, and top customers will require remembering two names.

And whatever your status, your profession may make it necessary to connect other information to an individual's face and name, such as their company, sales history, product details, and the like.

Don't I know you from somewhere?

Remembering names and faces is far more about remembering *names* and *linking* them to faces than having to remember both. We often *recognize* a face but just can't *recall* the name associated with it. So what we need to learn is how to get each face to *lead* us to the correct name.

As we discussed earlier, context may be a factor. A guy who had done some construction on my house over a period of weeks was invited to a wedding I attended. I realized I knew him when we met, but couldn't "place" the face at all. I didn't *forget* his face (and I quickly remembered the name as soon as I recognized who he was), but couldn't put the information together until I pictured his face in my home.

So before we discuss ways to use sound-alikes, rhymes, and vivid pictures to remember names, we have to create a mechanism to link the face with the name, to recall them *together*. That requires *attention*—taking the few seconds necessary to actually see the face before us, note and exaggerate (if necessary) some outstanding characteristic, and retain that picture in our mind. Then we can attach the name, via whatever mnemonic we choose, to the face.

Some people make it easy. Jay Leno's chin; Kim Kardashian's, ahem, posterior; or your brother's strange drooping mustache may need no enhancement to form a clear mental picture. For others, you may need to add a few strokes of the pen. Nice goatee? Make it extend to the floor. Bushy eyebrows could be growing like vines, oversized ears look like an elephant's, cheeks bulge like a chipmunk's.

How many facial characteristics can you recognize and exaggerate? After all, there are only so many prominent proboscises, dimpled chins, big eyes, and unique hairstyles. Won't you run out? Remember: Facial recognition is not usually the problem; *linking* names, titles, and other information *is*. It won't matter how many people you meet with the same large eyes or big noses or floppy ears, just as it won't matter how many are named Adam or Eve or Bud or Lou (as you will smartly use the same pictures for those—our original couple, Bud Abbott and Lou Costello).

Will you ever meet someone so inconspicuous that you simply can't exaggerate anything? Although I doubt it, in any such case you can just decide to focus on one feature, such as his or her nose, mouth, eyes, or ears. You will still have concentrated on the face—how else would you have noticed that there is, well, nothing to notice?—so you will still have made it memorable.

Nice to see you again, uh, guy!

As we are creating a distinctive picture of the face, we must also *listen* to and *repeat* the name out loud: "Hi, Frank. Nice to meet you." Now all we need to do is attach a large hot dog (for "Frank") to those bushy eyebrows. When we see him an hour or two later, we will immediately recognize his eyebrows and, when we do, see the hot dog growing from them. "Hi,

Frank! Nice to see you again." We "forget" many names because we just failed to actually "hear" them in the first place.

Repeating a name—and even asking a new acquaintance to repeat his or her name if you didn't get it—is the first step to *remembering* it. Of course, one can take repetition too far: My father used to address wait staff by name so many times in a single sentence that the entire family avoided heading to a restaurant with him.

I'm chopping up a rose with an ax...or burning it

With the techniques you've already learned in previous chapters to easily create outrageous pictures, many names will give you no trouble at all: Axl Rose, Rose Byrne, Tiger Woods, Mary Hart, Sean Penn, John Goodman, Jack Black, Whoopi Goldberg, and so on. In fact, you will be surprised how many names produce almost instant pictures because they are words you already know well:

Geographical terms: Kate HUDSON, RIVER PHOENIX, WOODY Allen, BROOKE Shields, Colin FIRTH, James WOODS, Jonah HILL, Albert BROOKS, LAKE Bell.

Metals: David COPPERFIELD, Freddie MERCURY, Emma STONE, Gracie GOLD.

Food: John CANDY, Jack LEMMON, Tim CURRY, Yun-Fat CHOW, Alison BRIE, Halle BERRY, Orson BEAN, Kevin BACON.

Tools: Jeremy IRONS, Peter O'TOOLE, Kristen BELL.

Countries: Willa HOLLAND, HOLLAND Taylor, Anatole FRANCE, Donna BRAZIL(e).

Animals: TIGER Woods, Megan FOX, Mardy FISH, Russell CROWE, Steve MARTIN, Ryan GOSLING, Laurence FISHburne, Ethan HAWKE, Jamie FOXX.

Cities: Rick SPRINGFIELD, Bryce DALLAS Howard, Whitney HOUSTON.

Flowers/trees: DAISY Buchanan, Orlando BLOOM, Chris PINE.

Gems: PEARL Buck, DIAMOND Jim Brady, Billy CRYSTAL, Keenan IVORY Wayans, JADEn Smith, AMBER Heard, RUBY Dee.

Colors: REDD Foxx, Seth GREEN, SCARLETT Johansson, James BROWN, Jack BLACK.

Drinks: TOM COLLINS, Mel GIBSON.

Occupations: Will SMITH, Bud ABBOTT, Chris COOPER, Grant TINKER, TAYLOR Swift, Ava GARDNER, Garry MARSHALL, Minnie DRIVER, Jude LAW, Christopher PLUMMER, Gerard BUTLER, Danny GLOVER, Hugo WEAVING, Elizabeth BANKS, Jennifer CARPENTER, Sienna MILLER, Rachael Leigh COOK.

Cards: QUEEN Latifah, JACK Nicholson, Don KING, Sam SPADE, Donald TRUMP.

Automobiles: Gerald FORD, Frieda PINTO, CHEVY Chase, Steve NASH, Harrison FORD, Richard GERE, Vin DIESEL.

Weapons: Nick CANNON, Peter GUNN.

I'm sure you will think of many more that are just as obvious and easy to use.

That president weighs a ton

Suffixes can trigger a picture, too. Any name ending in "*ton*" could suggest a "heavier" picture (an obese George Washington), while Wil*son* or Car*son* could suggest a smaller one. Picture an *angry* kiss (Henry Kissin*ger*) or an apoplectic fish (Kim Basin*ger*). Any name with a Mc or a Mac could make you picture a Scotsman, bag pipes, or a gooey Big Mac. A lot of toilets lined up with bagpipes sticking out? John McEnroe, of course—seriously!

Although you will find many names (especially first names) easy to picture, last names can be a struggle. Sound-alikes will work for many names: Sing for Vijay SINGH, Gelato for Lindsay GERRATO, Pachinko for Al PACINO, Cool lids for Calvin COOLIDGE.

And, as I have emphasized, you are free to use whatever pictures *you* find most memorable. If you are a sports fan, every TOM could be Brady, every WILLIAM or WILLIAMS Serena (or Venus!), every JASON Day, JORDAN Spieth, JOHN McEnroe, and on and on.

You can use celebrities for stand-ins with the same first or last names (KIM Kardashian, LINDSAY Lohan, BARBARA Streisand, CHARLIE Sheen). Or you can go farther afield: FRED Flintstone, BARNEY Rubble, BERT and ERNIE (plus FRAN and OLLIE), GEORGE Jetson, and so on.

Always use the images that work best for you. An art student may substitute Michelangelo's *David* for any person of the same name, picture every Sal as *Dali*, and every Andy as *Warhol*. Music buffs could decide every *John* is Elton, every *Billy* is Joel, and every *Mick* is a Jagger.

Your pictures certainly don't have to be famous. If you are on a sports team, you can use the faces of your teammates as your "touchstones," so every Chelsea is your third baseman, every Harriet your pitcher, and every Ginny your catcher. If you are in a sorority or fraternity, your sisters and brothers can be your key substitutes. Feel free to use the members of any club, association, or group to which you belong or any group of friends.

If you have to remember titles, just come up with a common picture: Every doctor gets a *stethoscope*, every professor is at a *lectern*, every judge is using a *gavel*, every senator is riding in a *hot air* balloon, and so on.

Oh, sure, just picture Yaveskova Krichmotovenurty

What if you are unable to come up with a mental picture quickly enough, or at all? If I met Fran Abromawitziac, I could picture her beautiful red hair with a *fan* atop it. And, given time, I could conjure up the biblical *Abraham with a sack* etched onto it. But alternatively, I could simply write, phonetically, the last name on the fan and be done with it. Difficult names can be written on foreheads in neon paint, inked onto a sign around someone's neck, hung from earrings on those large ear lobes—especially if you are meeting multiple people at once and simply can't take the time to do anything else.

If you are a sales professional, for example, you may have to remember even more information and link it to the person's face, whether pertinent family information (spouse's name, kids' names and ages and schools), company data (name, key products, sales history), or more. Although I think with very little practice you can easily meet and greet 50 or more new people by name at any gathering, trying to associate a large amount of additional data will take a lot more practice and, at some point, you will reach your individual limit. Storing some of that additional information, either by writing it down or entering it into your phone, may be necessary (and a good idea in any case).

Oh, yeah, your wife, What's-Her-Name

Again, the more you practice, the easier it will become. Let's presume you are a new salesperson attending a small social function. You have just been introduced to a new customer, Wayne Darby, a parts manager at Apple. While chatting, you learn about his wife, Kim, and his kids, Jordan, a high school football player, and Karen, who plays lacrosse. Wayne is an avid tennis player. They just adopted a new Shih Tzu puppy.

Whew, a lot to remember? Not really. Wayne has a memorable white pompadour. *Wayne* = wine and *Darby* = derby, so I would picture an upside-down derby (hat) on top of his head, overflowing with wine with an apple floating in it. His arm is around Kim Kardashian and they are talking to Michael Jordan, who is wearing a football helmet. Their Shih Tzu (I would picture Chubby, my own Shih Tzu!) is running through rows of lacrosse sticks dripping with carrots (Karen) and tennis racquets with large wine labels on them (for Wayne) sprouting from the ground.

You are not going to create this tableau in an instant, and it will take some practice to do so consistently, especially if you have to create a dozen or more in a single evening. So I still highly recommend that you find a way to transfer some of that information to a notebook, tablet, phone, whatever, as soon as possible. But as we've already seen, the more you *must* remember and the more you practice effective memory techniques, the more you *will* remember.

The list on the opposite page contains some fictitious (and harder) names to remember. What pictures and/or sound-alikes can you conjure up?

Cydnor Ticehurst

Ganesh Savarkar

Vladimir Ballentikoff

Zahoor Akhluq

Klas Linderlaught

Ossa Haramilloo

Manco Ypselqui

Lembert Quigg

Quentin Beukeldeau

Phelim Osterscholtz

Chapter 6

Remember More of
What You Read

*Some books are to be tasted, others to be swallowed, and
some few to be chewed and digested.*
—Francis Bacon

Let me state this up-front: *How **well** you learn something is far more important than how **fast** you read it.* A "smart" student may excel simply because he learns the material better, not because he has a "better" memory. He has learned how to *identify* and *organize* the *important* concepts, facts, and figures, and may be trying to remember far *less* than you.

Retention is primarily a product of what you understand. It has little to do with how fast you read, how great an outline you can construct, or how many fluorescent colors you use to highlight your textbooks. Reading anything, grasping the message, and remembering it are the fundamentals that make for high-level retention. Reading at a 1,000-word-per-minute clip does not necessarily mean that you understand what you read or will remember any of it.

If you really get the author's message—even if it takes you an hour or two longer than some of your friends—spending the time *you* require to understand what you are reading is key.

Listen to that Kindle in the Nook

Reading, of course, used to mean actual printed books. That has changed tremendously in the last two decades.

The original e-readers—Kindle, Kobo, Nook, and others—enabled you to read a digital edition of a book, and little else. The most current e-readers are actually tablet computers that include the pertinent digital architecture within them, allowing you to use features that may include a touchscreen, stylus, attachable keyboard, and so forth. As a result, you can now take notes, underline, highlight, color code, and otherwise mark up a digital edition.

If you already prefer a digital book to a printed copy, even if your normal slate consists exclusively of romance, sci-fi, and/or graphic novels, you will probably have no problem reading more serious literature on your tablet. Although many (but certainly not all) textbooks, magazines, journals, and newspapers are now available digitally, you may find their digital editions cumbersome or just not as easy to use. As long as you apply the advice in this chapter to your reading assignments, you may choose whichever format you prefer: print, digital, or, audio.

It's on the tip of my tongue

Recall is least effective immediately after a first reading, which is why reviewing the material later is so essential. You will remember only what you *understand*. When you read something and grasp the message, you have begun the process of retention. The way to test this is to rephrase the message in your own words. Can you summarize the main idea? Unless you understand what is being said, you won't be able to decide whether to remember or discard it.

You remember what you *choose* to remember. If you don't want to remember some piece of information or don't believe you *can,* then you *won't!* To remember the material, you must *want* to remember it and be convinced that you *will* remember it.

To really remember what you learn, you should learn material thoroughly, or *over*learn. This involves pre-reading, then doing a critical read, and having some definite means of review that reinforces what you should have learned.

It's more difficult to remember random thoughts or numbers than those organized in a pattern. For example, which phone number is easier to remember: 538-6284 or 678-1234? Once you *recognize the pattern* in the second number, it takes much less effort to remember than the first.

Develop the ability to discern the structure that exists and recall it when you try to remember. Have a system to help you recall how information is organized and connected.

It's helpful to attach or *associate* what you are trying to recall to something already in your memory. Mentally link new material to existing knowledge so that you are giving this new thought some context in your mind.

While we all have reasons to read *some*thing daily (and should), students in particular are *required* to read books covering a wide variety of subjects and need to be able to summarize what they have learned in an equally wide variety of test situations. So although many of the suggestions in this chapter apply to anyone trying to retain more of what they read, it is particularly relevant to anyone in school, whatever the level, whatever your age.

You must have a purpose

There are six fundamental purposes for reading:

1. To grasp a certain message.
2. To find important details.
3. To answer a specific question.
4. To evaluate what you are reading.
5. To apply what you are reading.
6. To be entertained.

Whether you are tackling a long newspaper or magazine article, a nonfiction book (biography, history, and so on) for pleasure, or an assignment for a particular school class, your approach to reading should be the same. Begin with a very quick overview, looking for questions that you'd like answered. Skim the pages to get a preliminary idea of what information is included. Then read the text carefully, word-for-word, and, if for a class, highlight, underline or take notes in your notebook, on your computer, or in the book itself.

Let's say you're reading a science book with the goal of identifying the function of a cell's nucleus. You can breeze through the section that describes the parts of the cell and skim the description of what cells do. You already know what you're looking for—and there it is in the section that talks about what each cell part does. Now you can start to *read*.

By identifying the questions you wanted to answer (your purpose) in advance, you would be able to skim the chapter and answer your questions in a lot less time than it would have taken to painstakingly read every word.

Skimming, or pre-reading, is a valuable step even if you aren't seeking specific facts. When skimming for a general overview, there's a very simple procedure to follow:

- ♥ If there is a title or heading, *rephrase it as a question*. This will be your purpose for reading.

- ♥ Examine all the *subheadings, illustrations, and graphics*, as these will help you identify the significant matter within the text.

- ♥ Thoroughly read the *introductory paragraphs*, the summary, and any questions at the chapter's end (in a textbook).

- ♥ Read the *first sentence* of every paragraph, which generally contains the main point of the paragraph.

- ✦ *Write* a brief summary that encapsulates what you have learned from your skimming.

- ✦ Based on your evaluation, *decide* whether a more thorough reading is required.

In textbooks, the heads, subheads, first sentences, and other author-provided hints will help you get a quick read on what a chapter is about. Some of the *words* an author uses will help you home in on the important points and ignore the unimportant. Knowing when to speed up, slow down, stop, or really concentrate will help you read both faster *and* more effectively.

When you see words and phrases such as "likewise," "in addition," "moreover," "furthermore," and the like, you should know nothing new is being introduced. If you already know what's going on, you can speed up or skip what's coming entirely. When you see words such as "on the other hand," "nevertheless," "however," "rather," "but," and their ilk, slow down—you're getting information that adds a new perspective or contradicts what you've just read.

Lastly, watch out for "payoff" words and phrases such as "in conclusion," "therefore," "thus," "consequently," and "to summarize," especially if you only have time to "hit the high points" of a chapter or if you're reviewing for a test. Here's where the author has tied up all the previous information in a nice bow. This unexpected present may help you avoid unwrapping the entire chapter.

As a general rule, if you are reading textbook material word for word, you probably are wasting quite a bit of time. Good readers are able to discern what they should read in this manner and what they can afford to skim.

If a more thorough reading of a text is required, go back to the beginning. *Read one section (chapter, unit, whatever) at a time.* As you read, make sure you know what's going on by asking yourself if the passage is written to address one of these five questions:

1. *Who?* The paragraph focuses on a particular person or group of people. The topic sentence tells you *who* this is.

2. *When?* The paragraph is primarily concerned with *time*. The topic sentence may even begin with the word "when."

3. *Where?* The paragraph is oriented around a particular place or location. The topic sentence states *where* you are reading about.

4. *Why?* A paragraph that states reasons for some belief or happening usually addresses this question. The topic sentence answers *why* something is true or *why* an event happened.

5. *How?* The paragraph identifies the way something works or the means by which something is done. The topic sentence explains the *how* of what is described.

Reading books about math and science

In most technical writing, each concept is like a building block of understanding: If you don't understand a particular section or concept, you won't be able to understand the *next* section, either. Most technical books are saturated with ideas, terms, formulas, and theories. The chapters are dense with information, compressing a great wealth of ideas into a few pages. They demand to be read very carefully, but you can take advantage of some common devices to make sense of the organization. Here are five basics to watch for:

1. Definitions and terms.
2. Examples.
3. Classifications and listings.
4. Use of contrast.
5. Cause-effect relationships.

In reading any specialized text, you must begin at the beginning—understanding the jargon particular to that discipline. Everyday words can have a variety of meanings, some of them even contradictory, depending on the context in which they're used. These same familiar words may have very precise definitions in technical writing. For example, the definition of elasticity (the ability of a solid to regain its shape after a deforming force has been applied) is the same in Denver or Djibouti. Such exact terminology enables scientists to communicate with the precision their discipline requires.

Definitions may vary in length. One term may require a one-sentence definition, others entire paragraphs, and some a whole chapter to accurately communicate their meaning.

Look for key words that indicate specific mathematical operations. You need to *add* when you see words such as "increased by," "combined," "together," "sum," or "total of "; *subtract* when you see "decreased by," "minus," "less," "difference"; *multiply* when you see "product," "increased," "by a factor of," and "times"; and *divide* when you see "per," "ratio," "quotient," or "percent."

Another communication tool is the example. Technical writing is often filled with new or foreign ideas—many of which are not readily digestible. They are difficult in part because they are abstract. Authors use examples to construct a bridge from abstract principles to concrete illustrations. These examples are essential to your ability to comprehend intricate and complicated theories.

Unlike other writing, technical writing places a very high premium on brevity in order to compress a great deal of knowledge into a relatively small space. Few technical texts or articles include anecdotal matter or chatty stories about the author's experiences.

A third tool frequently utilized in texts is classification and listings. Classifying is the process by which common subjects are categorized under a general heading. Especially in technical writing, authors use classification to categorize extensive lists of detail.

A fourth tool used in communicating difficult information is that of comparing and contrasting. Texts use this tool to bring complicated material into focus by offering a similar or opposing picture. Through comparison, a text relates a concept to one that has been previously defined—or to one a reader may readily understand. Through contrast, the text concentrates on the differences and distinctions between two ideas.

A final tool that texts employ to communicate is the cause-effect relationship, the fundamental quest of most scientific research. Science begins with the observation of the effect: What is happening? It is snowing. The next step is to conduct research into the cause: *Why* is it snowing?

Detailing this cause-effect relationship is often the essence of scientific and technical writing.

Cause-effect relationships may be written in many ways. The effect may be stated first, followed by the cause. An effect may be the result of several connected causes—a causal chain. And a cause may have numerous effects. If you're having difficulty reading such texts—or attempting to work out technical problems—try the following "tricks":

- Whenever you can, "translate" formulas and numbers into words. To test your understanding, try to put your translation into *different* words.

- Try to figure out what is being asked, what principles are involved, what information is important, and what's *not* important.

- Teach someone else. Trying to explain mathematical or scientific concepts to someone will quickly pinpoint what you really know or don't know.

- For long lists of items you simply must memorize—all the bones of the human body, a series of chemical formulas, basic scientific definitions—learn (or create your own) memorable acronyms, sound-alikes, links, stories, journeys, and palaces.

Become a critical reader

Words and writing have two levels of meaning that are important to your comprehension. The first is the literal or descriptive meaning. What a word expressly *denotes* means the specific, precise definition you'd find in the dictionary. Connotation involves the second level of meaning: the *significance* of the words. What does that mean? Beyond a literal definition, words communicate emotion, bias, attitude, and perspective. Analyzing any text involves learning to interpret what is implied, just as much as what is expressly stated.

Beyond grasping the meaning of words and phrases, critical reading requires that you ask questions. Here are 15 questions that will help you effectively analyze and interpret most of what you read.

1. Is there a clear message communicated throughout?
2. Are the relationships between the points direct and clear?
3. Is there a relationship between your experience and the author's?
4. Are the details factual?
5. Are the examples and evidence relevant?
6. Is there consistency of thought?
7. What is the author's bias or slant?
8. What is the author's motive?
9. What does the author want you to believe?
10. Does this jibe with your own beliefs or experiences?
11. Is the author rational or subjective?
12. Is there confusion between feelings and facts?
13. Are the main points logically ordered?
14. Are the arguments and conclusions consistent?
15. Are the explanations clear?

Chapter 7

Remember English Vocabulary and Spelling and Foreign Languages

Our borrowed mother tongue, English, is perhaps the most democratic of all languages. Built on a Celtic base, it has freely admitted a multitude of words from other languages, particularly French, Latin, Greek, German, and a rich body of slang (from anywhere we could get it).

The oldest branches in this diverse family tree, Celtic and Old English, are the least amenable to some of the techniques we are about to learn. These are basically simple words, not built in the complicated fashion of Latinate and Greek terms.

However, as anyone addicted to crossword puzzles can tell you, our language is replete with myriad Romance words (those from French, Italian, and Spanish) that often can be dissected into rather simple elements.

The following chart contains approximately two dozen roots from Latin and Greek that contribute to thousands of English words.

Root	Meaning	Example
annu	year	annual
aqua	water	aquarium
arch	chief	archenemy
bio	life	biology
cap, capt	take, seize	capture
chron	time	chronological
dic, dict	say	indicate
duc, duct	lead	induction
fact, fect	do, make	effective
fer	carry, bear	infer
graph	write	graphics
homo	same, identical	homonym
logos	word	logical
manu	hand	manufacture
mitt, miss	send	remittance
path	feel, feeling	apathy

ped, pod	foot	pedal
plico	fold	implication
pon, posit	place, put	imposition
port	carry	export
psyche	mind	psychopathic
scrib	write	scribe
spec	observe, see	speculative
tend, tent	stretch	intention
tene	have, hold	tenacious
vert, vers	turn	introverted

Prefixes, the fragments added to the beginning of a word, can greatly change the message conveyed by the root. The following chart contains examples of common prefixes.

Prefix	Meaning	Example
a-, ab-	from, away	aberration
a-, an-	without, not	amoral
ad-, af-, at-, ag-	to, toward	admonition, affection, aggressor
ant-, anti-	against	antidote
ante-	before	antecedent
bi-	two	bicycle
con-, com-	with, together	commitment

de-	away from	deviant
dis-	apart, opposite	disrespect
e-, ex-	out of, over	exorbitant
en-	in	envelope
extra-	beyond	extraordinary
hyper-	above, over	hyperthermia
hypo-	under	hypoglycemic
il-, im-, in-	not	illicit, impeccable
inter-	between	intercept
intra-	within	intrauterine
mal-	evil	maladjusted
multi-	many	multiply
ob-, op-	toward, against	obdurate, opposite
per-	through	perspicacious
peri-	around	peripatetic
post-	after	posthumous
pre-	before	premonition
pro-	for, forth	production
re-	again, back	regression
sub-, sup-	under	substantiate
sym-, syn-	with, together	sympathetic, synergy
tri-	three	triangle
un-	not	uncool

The last but certainly not the least important building block of words is the suffix, which quite often indicates how the word is being used. Suffixes can be used to turn an adjective into an adverb (the "-ly" ending), to compare things (smallER, smallEST), or even to modify other suffixes (live-LIEST). Some suffixes with which you should be familiar are:

Suffix	Meaning	Example
-able, -ible	capable of	pliable
-ac, -al, -ial	pertaining to	hypochondriac, remedial
-acy	quality of	fallacy, legacy
-age	quality of	outage
-ance, -ence	state of being	abundance
-ant, -ent	one who	student
-ary	devoted to	secretary
-cy	state of	lunacy
-dom	quality of, state of	martyrdom, kingdom
-en	made of	wooden
-er, -or	one who	perpetrator
-ful	full of	woeful
-hood	state of	neighborhood
-ic	pertaining to	pedantic
-ine	like	leonine

-ion	act of	extermination
-ish, -ity	quality of	purplish, enmity
-ist	one who practices	novelist
-ive	disposition of	active
-less	lacking	penniless
-ly	like	cowardly
-ment	process of	enlightenment
-ness	state of	holiness
-ory	pertaining to	memory
-ose	full of	grandiose
-ous	like	porous
-ry	state of	ribaldry
-some	full of	toothsome

I don't expect that you'll memorize these lists (though you probably could by now). But if you read them over a few times, paying particular attention to the examples, you'll absorb the roots, prefixes, and suffixes fairly quickly. As we saw in Chapter 3, forming your own associations—sometimes wildly outrageous ones—can be quite helpful in carving easy-access roads to our long-term memory banks.

In order to use this method, create a scenario using the sound-alike of the word or parts of the word and the definition of the word. Consider this example: Let's say that you've seen the word "ostracize" countless times, but can never quite remember that it means "to cast out from a group." You could then create either of these nonsense thoughts: "No one wants to look at the ostrich's eyes" or "The ostrich's size was so big he was thrown out of his hole."

Sure, you're saying, that's an easy example. So let's take another one. Because we're in a chapter on vocabulary, let's consider "sesquipedalian," which means "having many syllables" or "tending to use long words." Our sound-alike association could be: "She says quit peddling those big words."

If that doesn't seem to work for a particularly difficult word, one picture might be worthy of a particular vocabulary word. You might associate the difficult-to-remember word not with a phrase, but with an outrageous picture. For instance, to remember that the word "flambé" means a food that is set briefly on fire, think of a plate of food with bees whose wings are ablaze flying from it. Again, as we learned in Chapter 3, this sort of exercise is not a lot of work, but it is a great deal of fun. It'll help your mind hold onto words, even those you use infrequently, forever.

Here's a list of generally unfamiliar words with sound-alikes that will make them easy to learn:

- **Cutaneous** (pertaining to or affecting the skin): "Cute skin, ain't it just?"

- **Necromancy** (a method of divination through invocation of the dead): "Nancy, dig up Phil Niekro."

- **Hoosegow** (slang for a jail): "Whose cow is in jail?"

- **Welter** (to toss or heave): "Toss it here, Walter!"

- **Sullage** (sewage or waste): "Sully, age is a waste."

- **Hieromonk** (an Eastern monk who was also a priest): "Need a priest? Hire a monk."

- **Avouch** (to declare or assert): "'Ouch!' he vowed."
- **Cognomen** (a nickname or epithet): "No man was named Cog."
- **Dikdik** (a tiny antelope): "Did did you you see see that that antelope antelope?"
- **Guayabera** (a kind of Cuban sport skirt or jacket): "Put on your shirt and buy me a beer, Fidel."
- **Liatigo** (strap on a Western saddle): "Let that strap go, horsey!"
- **Petiole** (the stalk by which a leaf is attached to a stem): "Pet my old leaf."
- **Mizzle** (to rain in fine drops): "It's drizzling, Ma."
- **Jaguarundi** (a tropical American wildcat): "Jaguar undies on Top Cat!"
- **Frutescent** (shrubby): "Smelly fruits grew on the shrub."
- **Refrangible** (capable of being refracted, like rays of light): "Hey, Ray, ball the light for Angie."
- **Osteophyte** (an abnormal outgrowth of bone): "Two bones were fighting, Ossie."
- **Icosahedron** (a solid having 20 faces): "I guess he'd run 20."
- **Euclase** (rare green or blue mineral): "That green gem you got sure is classy."

Feel free to use *any* of the memory methods in this book to remember *any*thing. If you have to remember the word "surreptitious," which means secretive, stealthy, or sly, why not combine the sound-alike and chain-link methods to picture a burglar, black mask and all, carrying a bottle of pancake syrup?

I am sure some or all of the previously listed English words are as familiar to many of you as foreign vocabulary, so it should not be surprising that the same techniques—sound-alikes and outrageous pictures—will work just as well for learning any foreign language. Let's look at how we could remember some of the German words we used in the Chapter 2 quiz.

Esel (a donkey)	Picture a donkey painting on an easel.
Wissen (knowledge)	"I know I've had a vision" (the "w" is pronounced like a "v").
Obst (fruit)	"I'm abstaining from fruit."
Dorf (village)	As Hillary wrote, "It takes a Dorf!"
Geflugel (poultry)	Picture a large flugelhorn play-ing a chicken.
Rezept (prescription)	"Can I get a receipt for those pills?"
Zahn (tooth)	"My tooth is gone!"
Pilz (mushroom)	Picture a large mushroom atop a pizza slice.

What pictures or sound-alikes can you generate for the rest of that list?

Yes, spelling counts

One way to win the spelling bee in your town is to have a great vocabulary by using some of the suggestions mentioned earlier. Another way is to learn the rules of English spelling, then note the rather frequent exceptions to those rules. Although I would love to include such hints for a variety of foreign languages, that is beyond the capacity of this book.

Double consonants

Many people make mistakes on words with doubled consonants. The most common quick-repeating consonants are "l," "n," "p," and "s," but "t" and "r" repeat fairly often, too. Although the incidence of these doubles might seem accidental or arbitrary, they usually follow the following rules:

- 💡 Double "l": Usually results from adding suffixes ending in "l" to roots beginning with the letter and vice versa for suffixes (examples: *alliterative*, *unusually*). However, alien does *not* have a double "l" because it is itself a root.

- 💡 Double "n": A similar rule applies to "n"s. Double "n"s usually result from adding a suffix that turns an adjective ending in "n" into a noun (*wantonness* or *thinness*) or "-ny," which turns a noun ending in "n" into an adjective (*funny*).

- 💡 Double "p"s, "r"s, and "s"s don't generally have a hard-and-fast rule, so you'll usually have to rely on other tricks of memory. For instance, I've always had trouble spelling *embarrassment* (double "r" *and* double "s") because it certainly doesn't seem to follow the same rule as *harassment* (double "s" only). In these cases, you'll have to associate some rule with the word. When I worked as a reporter, I'd often hear people answer questions about spelling in such codes. "Four s's and two p's" is the answer to "How do you spell Mississippi?" I remember the rule for the word *harassment* by imagining someone pushing away (or harassing) the "r" my brain insists should be there (but isn't).

- Double "r"s and double "t"s and other doubles occurring (note the double "r"!) before "-ed": If the word ends in a single consonant (occuR, omiT) or if the word is accented on the last syllable (comPEL, reMIT)

Is it "i" before "e" or...?

The general rule is: "i" before "e" except after "c" or when it sounds like "a" as in neighbor and weigh. This rule holds, with some exceptions: *seize, leisure, caffeine* and the names of other chemical compounds.

Honest "-ab(l)e"

Many people get thrown over words ending in "e" that have "-able" or "-ible" added to them. What to do with that final "e"? *Keep* the final "e" for words ending in "-ice," "-ace," or "-ge." Someone is embracEABLE and situations are managEABLE. *Drop* that final "e" when it is preceded by any consonant other than "c" or "g" (*unlovable*).

Other rules for adding suffixes to words ending in "e" include:

- 💡 *Retain* the "e" when adding "-ly" and "-ment" (unless the word ends in "-dge." It's *judgment, not* judgEment).
- 💡 *Drop* the "e" before adding "y" as a suffix (*phony*).
- 💡 *Drop* the final "e" and add "-ible" to words ending in "-nce," "-uce," or "-rce" (*producible, inconvincible*).
- 💡 *Use* "-ible" for words ending in "-miss" (*dismissible*).

Its vs. it's

"Its" is the possessive of something (e.g., its color); "it's" is the contraction of "it is" or "it was" ("it's easy").

Your vs. you're

"You're" is used in place of "you are" (you're tall); "your" is an adjective (your grades).

Whose stuff is it, anyway?

If something belongs to each person, each person's name gets the "'s" (Jodi's and Dave's clothes, because they each have their own clothes), but if something belongs to people collectively, only the name closest to that something gets the "'s" (Jodi and Dave's house, because the house belongs to both of them).

Affect and effect

The general rule of thumb is that affect is a verb and effect is a noun. Because rules are made to be broken, though, effect is sometimes used as a verb.

💡 💡 💡

As I said at the beginning of the chapter, the English language is based on Celtic, Norwegian, German, Latin, French, and several other languages. As a result, it veers from the rules fairly often. So although these guidelines certainly will help you a great deal, sometimes you will have to rely on association and some of the other methods we spoke of in other chapters to remember all of the exceptions.

Chapter 8

Remember Numbers: Shapes, Rhymes, and the Major System

Up until now, we've been dealing in the rich world of words. Anything having to do with words is a relatively easy task for the memory because words can be associated with *things*. Because they can be seen, touched, heard, and smelled, they can carry more than one association and, therefore, be easier to remember. Even with minimal memory training, most of you could remember 26 words, even abstract ones, more easily and quickly than 26 random digits.

Unless associated with something, a number is relatively difficult to remember. For instance, most people have tremendous difficulty remembering telephone numbers that they've only heard once. The reason is that a phone number doesn't usually conjure up an image or a sensation. It is merely a bunch of digits without a relationship to one another or to you.

The trick, then, is to establish more associations for numbers.

As you discovered in the Chapter 2 quiz, you probably remembered no more than 10 random digits (unless, of course, you have undertaken some kind of memory training). If so, just a few minutes later, 10 would have devolved to six or seven. Tomorrow, it would be three, four, or even less. But with *minimal* training, you could easily remember all your important telephone numbers, every credit card in your wallet or purse (including expiration dates and security codes), your driver's license number, bank accounts, passwords, and much, much more. Although it may be much easier to simply assign "remembering" some of this to your phone, not all of you have glued it to your ear (yet) and not all such information should be online anyway.

Make zero a hero or a donut

The simplest way to translate a number into a word is to use rhymes:

0	=	Hero
1	=	Bun (Sun, Gun, Ton)
2	=	Shoe (Glue, Blue, Gnu, Sue)

3	=	Tree (Bee, Sea, Key, Pea, Tea)
4	=	Door (Floor, Boar, Roar, Soar)
5	=	Hive (Jive, Dive, Live)
6	=	Sticks (Hicks, Licks, Picks, Ticks, Bricks)
7	=	Heaven
8	=	Gate (Weight, Date, Bait, Mate)
9	=	Wine (Vine, Dine, Pine, Sign, Line)
10	=	Hen (Wren, Den, Pen)

If you actually were out and about without your phone and had to remember the phone number 877-872-6771, I am not sure how helpful this system would be—you'd be just two shy of 7th Heaven.

In order to make this system more useful, some have suggested adding additional rhymes, for example, "lever" (11), "elf" (12), and so on. But farther down the line, rhymes like "knighting" (19), "twin-ty" (20), and "gifty" (50) just seem weird.

Eight-time World Memory Champion Dominic O'Brien, whose eponymous system we will discuss in the next chapter, suggested another simple solution: replacing numbers with the shapes they represent: 0 is a ball, 1 is a pencil, 2 is a swan, 7 is a boomerang, and 9 is a balloon on a string (or a delicious donut). To memorize a 16-digit credit card number, you would need to create a story linking 16 pictures. This is certainly possible for you, but too limiting for me.

Turning numbers into sounds

One of the oldest number systems originated some 400 years ago and, though it's also simple, it is far more useful than the rhyme or shape systems. It has the added advantage of allowing words to represent two, three, or even more digits at a time. The following list shows you how each number is represented by a particular *sound*.

1	T or D
2	N
3	M
4	R
5	L
6	J, SH, CH, soft G
7	K, hard C, hard G
8	F, V, PH
9	P, B
0	Z, S, soft C

There is logic to this system.

- ♀ The number 1 is a single down stroke, as is the letter "T." "D" is a suitable substitute because it is pronounced almost the same way as "T"—by touching the tongue to the front of the roof of the mouth.

- ♀ "N" represents 2 because "N" has two down strokes.

- "M" is a stand-in for 3 because, you guessed it, it has three down strokes.

- The number 4 is represented by "R" because the dominant sound in the word *four* is the "rrrrrr" at the end.

- The Romans used "L" to represent 50. Also, if you fan out the fingers of your left hand as if to say, "It is 5 o'clock," your index finger and thumb form the letter "L."

- Hold a mirror up to a 6 and you get a "J," particularly if you write as badly as I do. Therefore, all letters pronounced like "J"—by touching your tongue to the inside of your lower teeth— are acceptable substitutes for 6.

- Place two 7s back to back, turning one upside down, and what do you have? Right, a "K." All letter sounds formed in the back of the mouth, as is "K," are therefore potential substitutes for the lucky seven.

- Draw a line parallel to the ground through a handwritten 8 and you will create a symbol that resembles a script, lower case "F." Therefore, all sounds formed by placing the top teeth on the lower lip can represent 8.

- Once again, a mirror will show you that a 9 and a capital "P" are virtually identical. "B," also formed by putting your lips together, is a substitute for 9 anytime.

- The number 0 is an easy one. It begins with a "Z," so any sound formed by hissing through

the space between a flat tongue and the roof of
your mouth is acceptable.

In addition, w, h, and y and all of the vowels—a, e, i,
o, and u—have no value and should be ignored, as are silent letters like the first "k" in "knapsack" or the "b" in
"tombstone." Double letters—the "ll" in "mellow" or "ss" in
"posse"—are only counted once, unless they are pronounced
differently, like the "cc" in "accident." "Q" as in "queen" or
"quick" is pronounced like a "k," as is the "x" in "fox" or
"except," so both, though rarely used, would represent "7."

So "**TiTL**e" would be a substitute word for 115—t =1,
then t=1, and l=5. The two vowels are silent. The number
85 could be "**FooL**." "**MoM**" or "**MaaM**" could represent
33, and she could be playing a "**VioLiN** (852) or **MahJoNG**
(3627).

Be sure you use the *sound* of the letter and not the letter itself to create your word: **ViC**e is 80, not 87, because
it is pronounced as an "s" sound, not as a "k" sound.
MaNSioN is 32**6**2, *not* 32**0**2. The "s" is a "sh" sound.

This simple but powerful system makes it much easier
to remember the number of that person you met in the mu-
seum today. Isn't it easier to remember "normal girl" than
243-5745 (NRMLGRL)?

How about trying to remember pi to seven places? You
could memorize 3.141592 or just think, "**My D**ea**R** Tai**L**
Bo**N**e."

Is it easier to remember your social security number (say,
143-25-7170) or "**D**oo**RM**e**N L**i**K**e **D**o**GS**"? Remembering
a phone number like 513-286-1562 is now as easy as remembering **L**e**T M**e**N F**i**SH T**i**L J**u**N**e.

Even memorizing a more intimidating 26-digit number like 16875832427999418509079858 is no longer quite as scary. Try grouping it into smaller number combinations, creating a picture for each:

168758 (TGFCLF) could represent **T**he ed**G**e o**F** a **CLiF**f.

3242779 (MNRNGCP): Standing there is a **MaN** wea**R**i**NG** a **CaP**. (Do you see him?)

9418509 (BRDFLSB: A **BiRD FL**ie**S B**y. What happened next?

079858 (SCPFLF): Hi**S CaP F**el**L** of**F**.

Of course, it will take some time to transform that long a number into a coherent sentence or story, and it is rarely efficient or easy to group six or seven digits together, as we just did. But this system is also helpful with word lists; you can now use it to memorize, say, 20 words *in order*. And once you do, you can then recall that list *in any order you wish*—front to back, back to front, and so on. This is a clear advantage over any link or story. This is also an easy way to remember *anything* in order—the steps to a complex recipe, the order in which states joined the Union or ratified the U.S. Constitution, the Ten Commandments, amendments to the U.S. Constitution, books of the Bible, steps in a chemistry experiment, steps in solving a complex math equation, and the like.

Rather than conjure up a different picture every time you have to remember "14"—"tire," then "door," then "tar" or "water" or "heater"—creating and memorizing your own list of *peg words* will be far more efficient.

Here are some possible peg words for numbers 00 to 20:

00	seas, Zeus, sauce, hoses
01	seat, soda, suit
02	sun, snow, swan
03	swim, seam, sum
04	sewer, czar, sore
05	sail, soul, soil
06	sage, sash, switch
07	sock, ski, sack
08	safe, sofa, sieve
09	soap, soup, spy
1	tie, toe, tee
2	Noah, hen, wine
3	Ma, emu, ham
4	rye, oar, wire
5	law, owl, wheel
6	shoe, jaw, witch
7	cow, key, hawk
8	ivy, wife, wave
9	bee, pie, oboe
10	toes, dice, toys

11	toad, tattoo, teeth
12	tin, dune, twine
13	tummy, dam, atom
14	door, tire, deer
15	doll, tail, outlaw
16	tissue, dish, dash
17	dock, deck, duck
18	dove, TV, taffy
19	tub, tape, tube
20	nose, noose, knees

I'm sure you can add to this list; it is certainly not exhaustive. My only caution would be to make sure whatever words you decide to use are easily transformed into pictures. Objects, therefore, work much better than verbs. Although you could use "wash" for "6," aren't the three previous suggestions easier to picture? While "nude" works for 21, I would personally prefer a knot, wand, or ant (or your favorite aunt). And objects that are easiest to picture will make your life easier as well—"rose," "horse," or "race" (all possible peg words for 40) are all superior to "warehouse" or even "hearse." "Chef" (68) is better than "java," "log" (57) better than "leak," and "daisies" (100) superior to "diocese" or "disease."

As these last examples illustrate, you can easily create your own peg words right up to 100. There are quite a few possibilities for most numbers. One way to make remembering 100 such words is to begin each group of 10 with the key letter the first digit represents. So words 30 through 39 would all begin with the letter "M" (3)—Mouse (30), Mud (31), Moon (32), Mom (33), and so on, even though you could have chosen to use Hams (30), Image (36), Hammock (37), or Imp (39). The peg words for numbers 40 through 49 would all start with "R" and those for 50 through 59 with "L," and so on. This small habit would be yet another aid to remembering your peg words.

I have included an abridged list of suggested peg words for all numbers 21 through 100 in the Appendix. Using these suggestions—and your own creativity—you may decide to create your customized peg word list right up to 100. Whatever words you choose, they should be most meaningful to *you*. If you are a gym rat, you can certainly picture your "lat" (muscle) for 51 and "gym" for 63. If you love milk shakes, what the heck, make 67 a "shake." Or remember your puppy by substituting "lab" for 59. Don't limit your imagination and remember that the strongest associations are made by tying new information to what you already know.

Without doing anything else, you could now remember two-digit "chunks" of information simply by picturing the appropriate peg words and linking them together. Five pictures would remind you of any phone number, eight any credit card number (plus four more for the expiration date and security code), and so on.

In their seminal *The Memory Book*, Harry Lorayne and Jerry Lucas suggest some added shortcuts to make easy transitions without having to think too much: If the peg word for 27 is "ink," then 270 is automatically "inks" (because 0 = s), 2727 is "inking" (27 = ng), 274 is "inker," and 271 is "inked."

Of course, various experts have devised ways to extend this system even further. Two-time U.S. Memory Champion Ron White has created peg words for all the numbers from 101 (**ToaST**) to 1,000 (**DiSeaSeS**), including interesting pictures like **FoaM** mou**T**h (833), **LuRe B**ag (549), and **InSuR**ance policy (264), again proving that your images only have to make sense to *you*. I have no idea what a Lure Bag is and am not sure I want to carry the picture of a Foam Mouth around in my head.

Others have found simpler ways to create new pictures for three-digit numbers. Dr. Kenneth Higbee, a psychologist and professor at Brigham Young University, suggests adding a descriptive adjective for all three-digit numbers to your pictures for two-digit numbers: wet for 1, new for 2, my for 3, hairy for 4, oily for 5, huge for 6, weak for 7, heavy for 8, happy for 9, and dizzy for 10. So 120 could be a "wet nose" or "wet knees," 333 could be "my mom," 486 could be "hairy fish," and 691, a "huge bed." Note that each of his adjectives follows the Major System—the "t" in "wet" for 1, the "n" in "new" for 2, the "m" in "my" for 3, and so on.

Six-time World Speed Memory Champion Ramon Campayo suggests a *location* in which to "place" each hundreds' digit: "1" is in a swimming pool, "2" in outer space, "3" is burning in hell, "4" is in your house, "5" is on a very dense planet, "6" is in the desert, "7" is at the North Pole, and so on. So if your peg word for 67 was "sheik," 167 would place him in a swimming pool and 467 in your house. 667 is, appropriately, a sheik in the desert.

On a side note, Campayo's readers should be aware that he has radically changed the Major System, with different sounds for the numbers 4, 6, 7, and 8, and a sound for 10. This may be because he takes part in contests to remember binary numbers (hence the use of a sound for 10, which no others use) or just to differ from the herd. Whatever the reason, don't try to compare the examples in his book *Maximize your Memory* (Career Press, 2010) to those used by Lorayne and Lucas, Ken Higbee, Dominic O'Brien, other memory authors, or me to explain the Major System. You will just get very confused!

Of course, if you rarely have the need to chunk numbers three at a time and are quite happy with your two-digit peg word pictures, you can create three-digit words as necessary to remember longer numbers when you have to. If your phone or a notebook aren't handy and you need to remember an important phone number—say 639-775-8510, you should be able to picture a **CHiMP JugGLing FLuTeS**.

Try it with some hypothetical credit card numbers, expiration dates, and security codes. You don't really want to keep that information on your phone or computer, do you?

4588 6312 9940 5588	Expires January 2019	Security code: 529
5286 9755 2820 4207	Expires December 2021	Security code: 667
5398 7730 1234 5678	Expires October 2022	Security code: 914

This system can be combined with other techniques to help you remember a wide range of facts and figures. How would you remember that the population of Nairobi, Kenya, is 3,138,369? Well, you could announce, "Nice robe, Kanye! It's a **MaDaM** (313) **FoaM** (83) **JoB** (69)."

If you had to remember that the earliest known compass was used in China around AD 1100, I'm sure you can find a way to link the compass in China to **ToaD SauCe** (1100); note that the latter is a far more effective picture (and taste!) than alternatives like **DaD's HouSe** or **DeaD ACeS.**

Here's a list of elements and their atomic weights. Can you create a sound-alike for the element, a peg word for the atomic weight, and a chain-link or story to remember them all? Feel free to change the order if that makes for a better story!

54	Xenon
49	Indium
74	Tungsten
33	Arsenic
107	Bohrium
25	Manganese
58	Cerium
31	Gallium
86	Radon
14	Silicon
50	Tin

In the next chapter, we will go into greater detail about two more advanced number memory systems. Take your time reading through these two chapters, then pick the system (or combination) that works best for you.

Chapter 9

Remember Numbers:
The Dominic and PAO Systems

Eight-time world memory champion Dominic O'Brien has devised his eponymous Dominic System using names (and faces) as initial peg words rather than the objects often used by others. Although it is surely a coincidence that the system bears his name, O'Brien claims that it is actually an acronym that stands for Decipherment Of Mnemonically Interpreted Numbers Into Characters.

Rather than basing his peg words on sounds, like the Major System, he initially uses letters to substitute pictures of *people* for numbers:

1	=	A
2	=	B
3	=	C
4	=	D
5	=	E
6	=	S
7	=	G
8	=	H
9	=	N
0	=	O

He suggests you start by picturing people you would automatically associate with a particular number: 25 could be Santa Claus, 10 could be Bo Derek (in the movie), 52 could be a picture of the King of Hearts (as in a deck of cards), and so on. You could add people associated with particular numbers that are meaningful only to you—my daughter's lacrosse uniform number (17), my wedding anniversary (24), my mom's birthday (31), and so on.

So then Einstein smashed the piano

Then, using the *initials* generated by his chart, you would fill in the peg words from 1 to 99. "15" translates to "AE," so you could use **A**lbert **E**instein (or **A**melia **E**arhart, **A**aron **E**ckhart, or **A**bba **E**ban). "11" (AA) could be tennis player **A**ndre **A**gassi (or **A**lan **A**lda, dancer **A**lvin **A**iley, or **Aa**liyah). 84 (HD) is **H**umpty **D**umpty (or **H**illary **D**uff or **H**ugh **D**ancy); 73 could be **G**eorge **C**looney (or **G**eoffrey

Chaucer or **G**raham **C**hapman); 81 could be actor **H**ank **A**zaria (or **H**enry **A**aron or **H**oratio **A**lger), and 33 is **C**lark **K**ent or **K**ato **K**aelin (with **O.J.** Simpson, of course, as 06), and so on.

As discussed previously, include those pictures that are most memorable to *you*—celebrities, TV stars, politicians, artists, musicians, athletes, cartoon characters, whatever. So 52 (EB) might be **E**mily **B**ronte for English majors, **E**rnie **B**anks for baseball fans, or **E**ubie **B**lake for jazz aficionados (among many other choices). Mix and match as you please.

Now if you had to remember a hypothetical 16-digit credit card number, you could create an eight-picture link in the example that follows. (I have chosen people with whom most of you will be familiar.)

44	11	27	21	99	41	58	26
DD	AA	BG	BA	NN	DA	EH	BS

I have decided that DD = Doris Day, AA = Andre Agassi, BG = Barry Gibb, BA = Ben Affleck, NN = Nick Nolte, DA = Dan Aykroyd, EH = Ernest Hemingway, and BS = Britney Spears. Can you link them together or create a simple story to do so?

Much like the peg words created to substitute for two-digit numbers in the Major System, this still requires linking a lot of pictures together, even if they are familiar faces. To make life a little easier, O'Brien introduced the Complex Dominic System, a way to remember any four-digit "chunk" by first picturing a *person* (the first two digits) then adding an *action and prop* (the second two). Andre (11) could be smashing a tennis ball, Dan (41) on the big screen, and Ernest (58) typing away, for example.

So 5252 could be Ernie batting a baseball. If you pictured Andre Agassi smashing a tennis ball for 11, then "1152" would be Andre hitting a baseball while "5211" would be Ernie Banks (or Emily Bronte or Eubie Blake) smashing a tennis ball.

That would simplify remembering our 16-digit credit card number on page 123. Rather than having to link eight pictures, we would only have to link four: Doris Day smashing a tennis ball (our action/prop for Andrei Agassi), Barry Gibb slapping Ben Affleck, Nick Nolte playing a conga drum (Babaloo!), and Ernest Hemingway singing into a microphone (perhaps not as tunefully as Britney).

I will never forget my anniversary again!

This new system would allow you to easily remember dates, translating the months (January as 01, February as 02, and so on) into your people pictures and adding the action/prop for the day. So November 15th would be busy Andre (representing the 11th month) writing an equation on a chalkboard (my action/prop for Albert Einstein, representing the 15th day). For February (the second month, represented by Odell Beckham, Jr.) 26th (Britney singing into a microphone), I would now picture Odell singing.

You could still choose other methods to remember important dates like birthdays, anniversaries, and anything else. March 6th—my wife's birthday—does not have to be written as 0306. Eliminating both zeros still creates a number—36—that can *only* represent the sixth day of the third month. And remembering 36 using the Major System is as easy as picturing my wife lighting a **MatCH**.

Eliminating the zeros only works, of course, for single-digit months (January through September) and the first nine days of each month. But even a date such as November 30th—my daughter's birthday—which transposes to 1130, can be represented by a vivid picture using the Major System: a colorful, sculpted circle of Native American **ToTeMS**. If you prefer to picture **A**lan **A**lda (11) performing an action on the prop for the person you have used for 30 (Clive Owen, Conan O'Brien, or even Carroll O'Connor), feel free to do so.

I think the greatest strength of the Dominic System is that some find it easier to picture people performing an action rather than a list of 100 separate objects (like in the Major System), although combining the two is pretty powerful. Having *three* separate mnemonics for each number makes the next system the most powerful of all.

The P(erson)-A(ction)-O(bject) System

For those of you who just can't get enough of numbers and want to use the most sophisticated system of all, there is the PAO System, which stands for Person Action Object. In this system, each number separately represents a person, his or her action, and an object, one step beyond the Complex Dominic System (which utilized both an action and a prop but didn't separate them). So now old Andre (11) smashing (11) a tennis ball (11) represents a *six*-digit number: 111,111.

If we represented 52 as Eubie Blake playing a piano and 15 as Albert Einstein writing on a blackboard, then we could represent a whole series of six-digit numbers:

11 52 15   Andre Agassi playing a blackboard

11 15 52   Or writing on a piano

15 11 52   Albert Einstein smashing a piano

15 52 11   Or playing a tennis ball

52 11 15   Eubie Blake smashing a blackboard

52 15 11   Or writing on a tennis ball

Just remember: Each six-digit chunk *always* has a two-digit Person performing a two-digit Action on (or to or with) a two-digit Object *in that order*. So 115215 is *always* your #11 Person performing your #52 Action on your #15 Object.

What do you do with your picture of Andre playing a blackboard? In other words, how do you now remember the various six-digit pictures if you have two (12 digits), five (representing 30 digits), or even more? Pick a room in your memory palace (or your front walk or garden or journey around town or on the golf course) and place one picture at each loci. *Voila!* My 12-loci front walk could now store 72 digits—enough to easily remember three 16-digit credit card numbers plus their expiration dates and security codes (with a couple of digits left over). And we have already seen how easily one can remember only a dozen pictures using loci.

So many choices, so little time

There are clearly different ways to set up your person-action-object sequences for 100 numbers (or even more): If you like the Complex Dominic System, you have already memorized a separate person, action, and object ("prop") for each number, so 100 distinct pictures, each consisting of *three* elements, are already available to you. You really shouldn't have to change anything, except perhaps to make each object or action a little more memorable on its own.

If you prefer the Major System, you can create your people using its sounds for first and last names (or single names that evoke the right picture): 11 could always be **T**im **T**ebow and 33 could be **M**oms **M**abley or **M**ary **M**artin or **M**rs. **M**iniver, but 15 could be (Salvadore) **D**a**L**i and 97 **B**i**G**gie Smalls. **CheR** could be 64 and **M**a**D**onna 31 (ignore the letters after the two that represent your two digits). Add an action and object to each. They do not have to go together—just because Andre wields a tennis racquet doesn't mean he has to be playing tennis with it. It might be easier for you to picture him wearing it or painting with it or baking it, or, for that matter, smashing a painting or water fountain rather than a tennis ball.

Finally, as a further aid to memory, some experts have suggested using the sounds of the Major System to tie together every person, action, and object. So 19 could be David Beckham typing on a tuba (t or d = 1, p or b = 9) and 44 could be Ronald Reagan roaring at an aurora (double r's everywhere). 77 (kk or cc or ck) could be King Kong cooking a cake and 82 Bono phoning heaven.

Whatever system you are using, even if it is "none of the above," making a logical (or, in some cases, a wildly *il*logical) connection among the person, action, and object will make each more memorable.

Do you have to be consistent? Not at all. Some of your people can be friends and relatives, others generated by the Major System, still others generated by the Dominic System. Does the number 2 conjure up a picture of a swan, as discussed earlier? Feel free to have it represent Wynona Ryder, Mila Kunis, or Natalie Portman, all stars of the movie *Black Swan*.

Was the summer so slow that you actually took the time to familiarize yourself with the portraits of every U.S. president? You can certainly use them as numbers 1 through 45. If the summer was *really* slow, you can add the vice presidents (just be careful, as there are some duplicates—don't use Ford, Nixon, Truman, and others twice).

As I have said before, it doesn't matter whether your final lists are particularly logical, meaningful, or memorable *to anyone else*, nor how you compiled them or what System you used, if any, to generate them.

If you are having trouble with any aspect of your own PAO System, just Google the term and you will easily find lists of thousands of famous names and objects and hundreds of actions to choose from.

Who could ask for anything more?

Unless you are angling on becoming the next World Memory Champion, using this two-digit PAO system, however you generate it, will enable you to do anything you need to on a daily basis, whether you want to remember all your credit cards and driver's license numbers, recall important scientific formulas and equations, or just astound your friends with your "magical" memory mnemonics.

And though many of the mental athletes taking part in national and international memory championships are using three-digit PAO Systems—memorizing *1,000* people, actions, and objects—Jones von Essen managed to win the world championship in both 2013 and 2014 using a two-digit system.

We talked about remembering important numbers like credit cards or passport numbers—those you don't really want to trust to your phone or computer—but there are a lot of other practical applications for your newfound number mastery.

If you were a student in a world geography class and had to study for a test on population growth, you would have no problem (after glancing at the following chart) remembering that Brazil's population was greater than Nigeria's, followed by Japan, Mexico, and the Philippines. Why? Because you just remembered your self-generated mnemonic **BuNJuMP**. But if you could actually quote the latest population figures for each country from memory, wouldn't *that* impress the teacher?

Brazil	204,259,812
Nigeria	181,562,056
Japan	126,919,659
Mexico	121,736,476
Philippines	100,998,378

Here's how I would start: Brazil's population is 20 42 59 81 2. Let's deal with the first six digits using our two-digit POA System. Your Person (20) could be former French President Nicolas Sarkozy (playwright Neil Simon, football coach Nick Saban, or Nancy Sinatra). The action for 42 is digging and the object for 59 is a blowtorch. (I'm just making those up, of course.) So your first clear picture is Monsieur Sarkozy digging a hole with a blowtorch. What do you do with "812," the three "extra" digits? Well, you could make up a word using the Major System—FuToN would work. Now we know what he's throwing in that flaming hole. Alternatively, we could use Higbee's method detailed in the previous chapter to transform a two-digit peg word into a three-digit one: 812 becomes "happy" (for 8) TaN (for 12).

Because all of the population figures are nine digits, we could also conceivably use Higbee's or Compaya's methods (same as the previous chapter) and create three three-digit peg words for each country's population. Using Higbee's method, Mexico's population could be remembered as a wet (1) net (21), weak (7) match (36), and hairy (4) cage (76). Campaya's would have the net in a swimming pool, the match at the North Pole, and a cage in your house. (If you like their approach but find "in the house" or "happy" not unique enough, feel free to create your own more memorable adjectives or locations.)

Try one or two methods on the population figures for Japan and Nigeria. Is one easier or faster for you than another? Create a few more nine-digit numbers of your own and practice whichever method works for you.

Why is Nicole Kidman in New York?

What if you have to remember the number of House representatives apportioned by state? Let's just consider 10:

Colorado	7
Wisconsin	8
Iowa	4
Connecticut	5
Hawaii	2
California	53
New York	27
Ohio	16
Maryland	8
Nevada	4

Would it be easiest for you to set them up in descending or ascending order? Alphabetically? Geographically? Just number them accordingly and use all the techniques you've learned to memorize the order of each state's representation, the state itself, and the number of representatives it has.

For example, if I have decided to remember the states in descending order of their representative totals, I could use my Major System object peg words to number them (either 1, 2, 3, or 01, 02, 03, as you prefer), use a picture of a prominent landmark of the state (or anything that will remind me of it), and a peg-word person to remind me of the number of representatives:

- Picture **L**ea **M**ichele (or Liza Minnelli or Leighton Meester)—53—surfing (for California) in a suit and tie (01) or with a huge big toe (1).

- Next, **N**icole **K**idman (27) is making a snow (02) angel at the foot of the Empire State Building (or drinking wine [2] while hanging off it).

- **D**wayne **J**ohnson (16) is swimming (03) or with my Ma (3) on stage at the Rock & Roll Hall of Fame (Ohio).

- **V**ince Vaughn (8), dressed in a navy uniform (Annapolis, Maryland), is rowing with a big oar (4) or falling into a sewer (04).

- The masked protagonist from the movie *V* (8) is throwing an owl in (5) (or sailing through—05) Green Bay (Wisconsin) stadium.

You may find Vince Vaughn and the movie *V* a bit of a stretch, but they would work for me. Could you use sound-alikes for the states, substituting cauliflower, Oh! Hi! Oh!, and so on? Certainly, though I think the pictures I have conjured up would make life simpler.

I've done the first five states in descending order. Can you come up with your own mnemonics for the rest of the list (in order): Colorado, Connecticut, Iowa, Nevada, and Hawaii?

Then look over the whole list again, put the book aside, and write all 10 states out in *reverse* order of their representation (just to show you how easy it is to do because of the way you have linked their order to a peg word).

If you have to remember any number, no matter how long, or, for that matter, any combination of letters and numbers—like a license plate, complex password, chemical formula, or mathematical equation—you now have all the tools you need to easily do so. We will look at some more of these examples in the next chapter.

Chapter 10

Remember Speeches and Oral Reports, Directions, Appointments, Dates, Equations, Formulas, and More

There is one thing most students and non-students have in common: At some point, everyone needs to make oral presentations of one kind or another. For students, that may mean reports on books, historical figures, or current events, or even speeches when running for various student-body, fraternity, sorority, or club offices. For non-students, your profession may demand periodic, even frequent, PowerPoint presentations, speeches, or reports to a handful of your colleagues or a banquet hall full of customers or clients.

There is nothing more frightening to most people—including death—than having to stand up and just "say a few words." I suspect we all share the fear that mid-sentence we will simply "zone out," remembering not a word of that brilliant speech we memorized just last night. However, there is no reason to fear public speaking of any kind. What you have already learned in this book will help you overcome that fear and confidently approach any speaking engagement.

And we *must*...uh...*have to*...um

Don't try to memorize any speech word-for-word. The "mind freeze" that sometimes occurs is deadly when you must remember to move seamlessly from word-to-word, rather than thought-to-thought or point-to-point. Stumbling on a single word can easily make you lose your place and, eventually, carom through the rest of your speech, erasing entire sections along the way.

For any presentation of any kind, here is the secret all great public speakers know: Tell them what you are going to say, say it, then tell them what you said. And rather than trying to memorize pages of text (or just reading it word-for-word, eschewing any connection to your audience), use an outline (a tool I am sure you learned at some point during school), then add to it the chain-link method we learned in Chapter 3: Reduce your thoughts and points to a tight outline, then create a simple word-and-picture story to remind you of each point.

For example, I recently had to give a speech in front of a local high school's athletes and their parents, celebrating the record-breaking season of the girls' lacrosse team I coach. I needed to make the following points:

1. Thanking the school principal, athletic director, and team parents.

2. Citing the litany of obstacles (injuries, weather, key players quitting mid-season, and so on) the team had to overcome.

3. How the team overcame those obstacles and the results they achieved.

4. The importance and contributions of the three seniors on the team.

5. Individual letters and awards.

As we have learned, the more you already know about a subject, the easier it is to add new information. I knew this team and the players well, but there was still a lot of information that I wanted to include, and I didn't want to forget any of the specific honors or milestones individuals had achieved.

The outline identified the five sections of my speech, so all I had to do was make sure I linked each section together, while also ensuring I forgot none of the details. For the first section, I pictured Richard Nixon (yes, "Nixon" was the principal's name) shaking hands with the athletic director and team parents. I needed no reminders of their names.

The second section was made easier because most of the obstacles I was highlighting involved particular girls—Chelsea spraining her ankle, Jen tearing her ACL, and Sammy leaving the team on the second day. I used my ubiquitous walkway to remember them in order by picturing Chelsea with a huge ankle leaning against the first post in front of my house, Jen laying across the top of the right-hand post with an exploding knee, and then Sammy standing at the mailbox waving good bye. It was easy to remember the half-dozen other injuries and events, in the order they occurred, by simply adding them to my "walk." A thunderstorm was raging during my walk, so I remembered to talk about the weather at the end of the section. (Doesn't it make sense to use the Loci system invented by Roman orators to *remember speeches* when *you* have to give a speech?)

The third and fourth sections were all pretty easy, but the fifth required remembering various awards, records set, and milestones achieved. Using peg words and clear pictures made remembering all of those details a snap: Anyone who made first-team All Conference was wearing a Tie (1) and second teamers were wearing a Nun's habit (2), clearly a remnant of my Catholic upbringing. Chelsea, the MVP (written in neon on her tie) was Kno**CK**ing over a record player (77 goals that season, a school record). Senior Elaine was having **DiNneR** (representing her 124 career goals). Because I could readily picture each of the players, I could attach any number of peg words (and picture them) to each one and easily remember a long list of pertinent statistics.

By dividing my speech into five distinct sections, then applying the mnemonic techniques we have learned to fill in the details, I was never in danger of "losing my place" and never at a point where a forgotten word or phrase would leave me staring blankly at a quiet audience. (If you *do* stumble, remind yourself that the pause you *think* dragged on forever was barely noticeable, if at all, to most of your audience.)

Some of the presentations or speeches you may have to prepare may be more involved, longer, or require many more links to remember product details, sales points, or a lot of numbers. But you have learned how to deal with all of these situations in the previous chapters. So although it may take you longer to create the links, sound-alikes, and pictures, you need to follow your outline and remember everything you want to say, but it will *not* require you to do anything you don't already know how to do.

There are a surprising number of instances in which your ability to easily remember words and numbers, in order or not, will come in handy. My example used just a few practical applications of the many techniques you have learned.

Technology has made some of these chores (memorizing your calendar, directions, or complex passwords) so easy there is rarely a need to count on your memory. But, as they say, stuff happens.

So I take a right, no, a left, and then, oh, no...

I am a staunch believer in Google Maps and would wind up in a ditch somewhere without it, but if you aren't really sure where you are going, it will not get you there.

Given your newfound mnemonic memory, there is no reason you have to rely on your smartphone, navigator, or any other electronic device. Let's say your phone just died and you are lost on a back-country road. A helpful stranger knows just where Aunt Patty's Antique Barn is. Just follow these simple directions: "Go straight for about a mile, then turn right at the old henhouse, then make a quick left at the church. Go another two miles and take a right at the third traffic light, then a left at the next light. Straight for about three miles and there it is on your right."

I have been in that situation, listened attentively, nodded dully, and then proceeded to forget everything after "go straight" seconds after accelerating. But there is an easy way to translate those directions. First, though, we need to create a mental picture for "left," "right," and "straight." "Left" for me is a referee in full gear pointing me left; my old friend Greg Wright always tells me to go right, and if I see neither of them, I presume I am just going straight.

So here is the mental picture I would use to follow those directions: My friend Greg is shouting "we're number one" and is waving to me as I come upon an old henhouse. So I turn right, and immediately see the referee in front of the church pointing left. After driving for a while, I see my friend Greg mowing (m = 3) a light and know that is where I am supposed to turn right. Up ahead, there's my referee drinking tea (T = 1) and I know to turn left. I know to just go straight until I see my friend Greg on the right side of the road. I don't need to remember that it is a three-mile drive at that point.

That's a scenario that works for me. Would it work for you? Would you prefer different, more unique pictures? Or do you prefer to put each individual direction at one loci in your Memory Palace? Feel free to utilize whatever method is most comfortable to you. The key takeaway is that you *can* remember even complicated directions when you no longer have a technological aid. And you have a wide variety of memory tools from which to choose.

Ah, yes, that would be a Tuesday

With thousands of calendar and scheduling apps for your smartphone and a wide variety of trusty paper calendars and appointment or assignment books, there is rarely a time you will need to name a particular day of the week months from now and "pencil in" a new appointment. This was a more useful memory tool a couple of decades ago (when many of the best-known authors released their books). But if it ever does happen, here is a way to do so (and if it doesn't, a way to impress your friends with your astounding mental powers): Just remember 266 315 374 264, the number that represents the first Monday of each month in 2017 (January 2, February 6, March 6, and so on). And how would you remember *that?* Why not divide the 12 digits into two groups, then apply the PAO System to them?

Let's say you have used the Major System to establish the following person, action, and object for each two-digit number, as follows:

26	Nick Jonas is beating a Wench
63	John Mayer is ringing a Chime
15	Demi Lovato is tearing up a Towel
37	Mila Kunis is snoring in a Hammock
42	Richard Nixon is eating a Heron
64	Julia Roberts is shooting at a Jar

So our number would translate into two pictures: Nick Jonas is ringing a towel (26 63 15) and Mila Kunis is eating a jar (37 42 64).

Now what day is June 20th? The first Monday is the 5th, so two Mondays after that (14 more days) is the 19th. The 20th is a Tuesday.

What about making a doctor's appointment for that day at 10:30? Just picture Dr. Seuss (1 = D, 0 = S) wearing a stethoscope made out of hams (3 = M, 0 = S). You could easily remember a few such appointments—at least until you retrieved your phone or appointment book and could write them down. There would certainly be no need to remember them thereafter.

Remembering complex passwords

One hopes that most of you do not use your birthday or anniversary or dog's name as your "go-to" password for all your online accounts. It would be smart to use a series of more complex passwords devised in such a way that you will never forget them. Here's one idea:

85P47I63E!

Feel free to substitute any numbers (as long as you use PIE or some other easily recognized three-letter word). Then, using the PAO System, create a single picture for the six-digit number you have used. In this case, that might be Frank Langella (person for 85) whipping (action for 47) jam (object for 63). What about the letters? I would think it easy to remember PIE (or any other easily pictured three-letter sequence, like Elk, Gym, Bud, Cat, and so on) if you put it in neon letters. Whatever symbol you wish to use at the end (or anywhere else) could be attached however you choose to the Pie, Elk, Gym, and so on. Could you remember five or six or more such passwords just with a single picture and a neon word? I think so! And any such password is going to be a lot stronger than "123456" or "Sally."

Combining techniques as you wish works for a lot of number and letter combinations. My daughter remembered the license plate of her first car (N33DHD72) by combining an acronym with Major System peg words: **No MoM (33) Don't Hit Dad aGaiN (72)**. This is also a way to remember any driver's license that consists of a variety of numbers and letters. If it is all numbers, any system from the previous two chapters would work by itself.

Remembering chemical equations, formulas, or laws

Slogging through physical chemistry during my first year of college, I have never felt more lost in any class, before or since. And no memory techniques, no matter how advanced, could have helped me when the first textbook (out of 10) began: If (followed by a two-line equation) or (another) but (yet another), then (some other one)," and so on for a couple of hundred pages. It will be a great chore to remember a long series of equations or formulas no matter how much you practice using mnemonic techniques. And the more complicated they are, the more difficult they will be to remember.

BUT if you keep forgetting an equation like $K = 1/2 mv^2$ (kinetic energy is one half times mass times the square of velocity), the mnemonic techniques you have learned will help you remember it (and many others like it) *long enough to write it down the minute you enter the classroom*. And you can jam a few such equations into your brain if you only need remember them for a short time. Let's picture a **K**ing (with only the top **half** of his body in a car (**m**otor **v**ehicle) with a hen (2) squawking on the roof. Simple, memorable, effective.

How could we remember Newton's Three Laws of Motion?

1. Every object in a state of uniform motion tends to remain in that state of motion unless an external force is applied to it.

2. The relationship between an object's mass (m), its acceleration (a), and the applied force (F) is $F = ma$.

3. For every action there is an equal and opposite reaction.

Do we need to remember these word for word? Of course not. We just need to be able to recall the meaning of each law. The first law is essentially the definition of "inertia" (and is sometimes just called the Law of Inertia). So let's just remember "Inner Shah." Or picture your lazy brother sound asleep while his alarm keeps ringing!

The second law could conjure up a picture of my father (F) and mother (ma) looking at each other from opposite ends of a set of parallel bars. Having studied these laws, if I remembered $F = ma$—which this picture would help me do—I wouldn't need to remember anything else.

I would now picture my father and mother pushing off from their respective ends and falling away from each other.

Voila! An easy way to remember all three laws. Are there other techniques you could use? Always feel free to choose whichever ones work for you.

How about remembering something like the formula for benzene (C_6H_6? Well, "Ben seen Cash Hash" reminds me of Benzene first, then the "sh" sound tells me there is a subscript of 6 after the C and another 6 after the H. Because many chemical formulas use carbon (C), hydrogen (H), oxygen (O), and nitrogen (N) atoms in various combinations, making your own system to utilize these letters in your pictures will surely aid you. If you are taking a chemistry course, you should also already know that there aren't any molecular formulas that use superscripts, like squared (^{2}) or cubed (^{3}). Numbering of atoms always involves subscripts, like H_2O.

For sulphuric acid (H_2SO_4), picture a volcano spewing **H**ot **N**oses (2) that land at a **S**ewer (suggesting the S for sulpher but also the peg word for "04"). Its molecular weight (98.079) you could remember as Beef (98) Sock (07) Pie (9), using Major System peg words.

The more scientific or mathematical equations, laws, and formulas you are trying to remember, the more helpful it would be to find picture substitutes for the most-used symbols. You could picture parallel bars for the equal sign, a big checkmark for square root, numbers (or pictures they represent) rising or sinking into the ground (for superscripts like mv^2 and subscripts like H_2O), and even create substitute words for "squared," "cubed," and the like.

Columbus sailed the ocean blue in 1492

Students in many courses need to remember events and dates. But even if you are no longer a student, being able to remember birthdays, anniversaries, and upcoming events and dates would be helpful. We have already learned all of the techniques we need to do so.

Let's see how easy it is now to remember a few of the Civil War dates and events we included in Chapter 2:

May 12, 1863	Battle of Raymond
May 25, 1862	Battle of Winchester
July 1, 1863	Battle of Gettysburg
April 12, 1861	Battle of Fort Sumter
March 8, 1862	The Battle of Pea Ridge
September 18, 1863	Battle of Chickamauga

We need to remember the month (01-12), day (01-31), and year (61-63) for these six battles. (Because we know each occurred in the 19th century, we can omit the "18" from each year. This enables us to use the PAO system for these dates:

05 12 63

05 25 62

07 01 63

04 12 61

03 08 62

09 18 63

The people we would use are Spike Lee (05), Stephen King (07), Smokey Robinson (04), Seth Meyers (03), and Steve Buscemi (09). The objects are a gym (63), chain (62), and jet (61). Whatever actions would be associated with the days—12, 25, 01, 12, 08, and 18—would be filled in accordingly. Here are a few examples that I made up.

So we could picture Spike Lee jumping in the gym for the Battle of Raymond. That was the name of my favorite uncle, so I would add him to the picture. Or you could use a sound alike and have Spike wearing Ray-Ban sunglasses.

The Battle of Winchester clearly brings a rifle to mind, which finds its way into my picture of Spike, again, knitting a chain (perhaps attached to the rifle)?

How would you remember the other battles and their dates?

Keep in mind that you should always look for shortcuts. If you know various events you are studying all took place in the 20th century, leave out all the "19"s; if you are studying the Revolutionary War, eliminate the "17"s from the dates.

This same concept could be easily applied to make sure you never forget anyone's birthday or, perish the thought, your wedding anniversary. Just use the birthday girl or boy as the person in your PAO system, with the action of the appropriate month (01-12) and the object of the day (01-31). If you need to remember month, day, and year, use your "regular" person, action, and object from your two-digit PAO System and then just incorporate the birthday person into the picture, holding hands, holding the object, laughing at the action, whatever.

For anniversaries, just picture your charming spouse (or parents or married children or friends) in place of the person and add the appropriate actions and objects for the months and days.

For the card sharps among you

Key contests at national and world memory championships involve cards—how fast someone can memorize a single deck and how many decks can be memorized in 15 minutes, 30 minutes, or an hour, and so on. Because only a tiny fraction of you are reading this book in order to learn what you need to compete at such events, I will only include a brief discussion of how to remember cards. After all, there are a lot of bridge, blackjack, gin rummy, and poker players out there who will find it helpful. (Though becoming an expert at counting cards will get you ejected from most casinos, but that is a discussion for another time.)

The easiest system I have seen was suggested by Harry Lorayne and Jerry Lucas in *The Memory Book*. They suggest creating Major System peg words that immediately tell you both the suit (diamonds, hearts, spades, or clubs) and value (2–10, jack, queen, king, ace). So for diamonds, here are their suggestions:

Ace	Date
2	Dune
3	Dam
4	Door
5	Doll

6	Dish
7	Dock
8	Dive
9	Deb
10	Dose

The suit of each card is immediately obvious—every word starts with "D" for diamonds. And the words follow the sounds of the Major System—the "t" for 1, "n" for 2, "m" for 3, and so on. The same system for all aces through 10s can then easily be applied to spades (suit, sun, sum…), hearts (hat, hen, hem…), and clubs (cat, can, comb…).

The jack in each suit is the image of the suit—a diamond, heart, spade, or club. The pictures for queens and kings start with the first letter of the suit and then rhyme with queen or king, so the king of spades is "sing" or "sting," the king of clubs is, well, "king." The queen of diamonds is "dream" and the queen of spades is "steam."

Decide beforehand how you will order the suits in your memory—alphabetical (clubs, diamonds, hearts, spades), highest to lowest ranking (spades, hearts, diamonds, clubs), lowest to highest (clubs, diamonds, hearts, spades), or whatever other system works for you.

Kevin Horsley suggests essentially the same system in his book *Unlimited Memory* while changing some peg words, not always for the better—"camo" for "comb," and "Dan" for "dune," for example. And Dominic O'Brien suggests using *his* system to create the pictures you need, so the ace of clubs could be Al Capone and the 8 of hearts could be Hulk Hogan.

You can certainly replace some peg words with others, as Horsley chose to do, as long as you maintain the integrity of the system. And if you are already comfortable using the Dominic System to remember random numbers, you may, of course, continue to do so to memorize cards.

Lorayne and Lucas also offer an alternative set of peg words for jacks, queens, and kings (the "court cards") that continue the Major System pattern, such as "cuTe Ma" for the king of clubs—the "t" and "m" indicate the 13th card in the suit—or saTiN, indicating the 12th card in the spade suit, the queen. If that makes sense to you, adopt it.

Once you have settled on your peg words, strengthen the specific pictures each produces in your mind. Then practice turning over a deck of cards, one by one, and see how little time it takes before you can remember the order of all 52 cards by creating a story using your peg-word pictures.

There are times and games in which it is important for you to know exactly what cards have already been played. In gin rummy, for example, you would want to know whether your opponent is collecting 8s before you discard one. In poker, you would benefit by knowing that four aces have already appeared—so trying to draw an ace for your straight is impossible. As each card is played, just picture it exploding (or catching on fire or being torn up). If three aces have already gone up in flames, you at least have one chance for that straight!

I think you will find it surprisingly easy to use this method the next time you need to either remember the 26 cards that your opponents at the bridge table are hiding from you or all the cards already played (and not just the trump suit).

Poker or single-deck blackjack players will also find such a simple system easy to use to calculate odds at any moment of play. And, of course, there is always the chance to surprise your friends with yet another of your newfound memory skills!

I could add other areas in which you could utilize all the new memory skills you have developed, such as memorizing long lists of books and their authors, musicians and their songs or albums, artists and their works, sports, plays, musical chords, any combination of numbers and letters or words and numbers (like product codes and prices), and many, many more. Feel free to come up with your own challenges and apply your new skills. I think you will be suitably impressed.

Chapter 11

Never Fear Tests Again

As important as they are, the many memory techniques in this book are the study ingredients *least* likely to be taught in schools, even in a study skills course. So although many schools and teachers might help you with reading, writing, organizing, and test strategies, far too many of them will still "forget" to help you with your memory.

There are certain aspects of memory that are especially important when you are facing a test, whether you are a student dealing with midterms or finals, or a professional taking a licensure or certification exam, the bar exam, or medical boards.

In any such case, *stress will affect your memory*.

How to reduce your anxiety

The more you know about the test, the more you can concentrate on (and remember) only the material you need:

- ☼ What material will the exam cover?
- ☼ How many total points are possible?
- ☼ How much time will I have to take the exam?
- ☼ Where will the exam be held?
- ☼ What kinds of questions will be on the exam (matching, multiple-choice, essay, true/false, and so forth)?
- ☼ How many of each type of question will be on the exam?
- ☼ How many points will be assigned to each question?
- ☼ Will certain types of questions count more than others?
- ☼ Will I be penalized for wrong answers?

If your mind is a jumble of facts and figures, names and dates, you may find it difficult to zero in on the specific details you need to recall, even if you know all the material backward and forward. The adrenaline rushing through your system may just make "instant retrieval" impossible.

The simplest relaxation technique is deep breathing. Lean back in your chair, relax your muscles, and take three very deep breaths (count to 10 while you hold each one).

There are a variety of meditation techniques that may also work for you. Each is based on a similar principle: focusing your mind on one thing to the exclusion of everything else. While you're concentrating on the object of your meditation (even if the object is a nonsense word or a spot on the wall), your mind can't think about anything else, which allows it to slow down a bit.

The next time you can't focus during a test, try sitting back, taking three deep breaths, and concentrating for a minute or two on the word "RON." When you're done, you should be in a far more relaxed state and ready to tackle the next section.

A friend of mine once took the LSAT (Law School Admission Test) and did pretty poorly. But he wound up getting accepted to his top choice anway. Because he had already signed up to take it again—and paid for it—he retook a test that meant essentially nothing to him—and destroyed his previous score. The simple act of convincing yourself that the test is not as important (as you know it really is) may help you relax.

Never study everything

Once you've discovered the type of test you are facing, you need to figure out what's actually going to be *on* it (and, hence, what you actually need to study). Remember: It's rarely, if ever, "everything."

Conduct a cursory review of the material you are convinced is not important enough to be included on an upcoming test. This will automatically give you more time to concentrate on those areas you're sure *will* be included.

Then create a "To Study" sheet for each test. On it, list specific books to review, notes to recheck, and topics, principles, ideas, and concepts to go over. Then check off each item as you study it. This will minimize procrastination, logically organize your studying, and give you ongoing "jolts" of accomplishment as you complete each item.

As we discussed early in this book, our short-term memory is severely limited in time and space, so very little will be retained there, even minutes after studying. Though we have learned many ways to more easily transfer what we want and need to remember to long-term memory, it is also important to point out how we can make those memories stronger and make their retrieval easier.

The key is spacing—spreading one's efforts out in a pattern that many studies have now shown does exactly that. If you are studying for a test that is a month away, you should review *tomorrow* what you studied *today*, then again in three days, again in a week, then weekly until your test. Each time, of course, you will probably be spending less time going over the same material, but the mere act of reviewing it yet again is making its "tags" or "codes" *stronger* and the facts and figures *easier* to retrieve. The farther in the future the test, the longer the review intervals can become.

How you actually spend that review time is also key. It is awfully easy to reread the same material for the third, fifth, or seventh time and convince yourself that you are "reviewing" it, when you are really just listlessly thumbing through pages while thinking about...everything else.

If you have allocated four hours today to review a particular course, better to spend only two hours *today*, then two hours *tomorrow* or, even better, two hours the *day after tomorrow*. Each time you return to the same material, you are forced to reengage with it, strengthening your associations. You can easily test this assertion. Make a list of 10 relatively obscure authors and their works and a second list of 10 unfamiliar artists and their most famous paintings. Study the first list for 10 minutes today and 10 tomorrow. Study the second list for 20 minutes today only. In three days, try to recall both lists. I think you will find you do far better with the first than the second.

The way to strengthen your mastery of the material even more is to replicate the test you are facing, either by asking yourself questions about the material or doing so with friends in a study group. Even if you don't know the answers and have to keep searching through your texts to find them, the mere act of self-testing is a proven way to increase your recall. Some studies suggest that more than *half* of your test preparation time should be devoted to self-testing. Their theory is that just reviewing notes or highlighted texts is an inherently *passive* process, whereas a self-test requires your brain to *actively* seek out memories, strengthening your associations, and links.

My daughter's medical school experience has born this out. She has definitely found that a couple of courses in which she faced only a final exam (at the end of a three-month semester) presented far more challenges than those in which she was tested more often, even one or two in which she was quizzed weekly. Each of those quizzes, she found, not only made the material more memorable, but acted as the positive (or negative) feedback she needed to judge her progress and adjust her studying. With so many quizzes to look back on at the end of the semester, her review for the final exam was easier, quicker, and resulted in better grades.

The harder you make your self-tests, the better prepared and more confident you will be when you confront the real thing. Practice tests offer some real advantages, whether you're studying for a weekly quiz, the SAT, or your bar exam. In fact, the longer and more "standardized" the test, the more important it is to be familiar with its structure, rules, and traps.

Familiarizing yourself with the type of test you're taking will enable you to strategically study the material (prioritize) and strategically attack the test (organize). Familiarization breeds comfort and being comfortable—*relaxed*—is a key component to doing well.

Familiarization also breeds organization, allowing you to concentrate on the test itself and not on its structure. This gives you more time to actually *take* the test rather than figure it out. It also reduces the effect of whatever time constraints the test imposes on you.

Cramming doesn't work

We have all done it at one time or another, with one excuse or another: waited until the last minute and then tried to cram a week's or month's or entire semester's worth of work into a single night or weekend. Did it work for you? I didn't think so.

The reality is that cramming works—on one level—for a small minority of students. Somehow, they're able to shove more "stuff" into short-term memory than the rest of us and actually remember it, at least for a few hours.

The rest of us don't even get that smidgen of good news—after a night of no sleep and too much coffee, we're lucky if we remember where the test *is* the next morning. Some hours later, trying to stay awake long enough to make it back to bed, we not only haven't learned anything, we haven't even done very well on the test we crammed for!

That's probably the best reason of all not to cram: It probably *won't* work! And remember: Reviewing one last time before an exam is not cramming; it is reinforcing previous learning trying to learn the material for the first time.

How to cram anyway

Nevertheless, despite your resolve, best intentions, and firm conviction that cramming is a losing proposition, you may well find yourself—though hopefully not too often—in the position of needing to do *some*thing the night before a test you haven't studied for at all. If so, there are some rules to follow that will make your night of cramming at least marginally successful:

- 💡 **Be realistic about what you can do.** You absolutely *cannot* master an entire semester's worth of work in a single night, especially if your class attendance has been sporadic (or non-existent) and you've skimmed two books out of a syllabus of two dozen. The *more* information you try to cram in, the *less* effective you will be.

- 💡 **Be selective and study in depth.** The more classes you've managed to miss and assignments you've failed to complete, the more selective you need to be in organizing your cram session. So you must identify, as best you can, the topics you are sure will be on the test. Then study only *those*. It's better in this case to know a lot about a little rather than a little about a lot. You may get lucky and pick the three topics the three essays cover!

- 💡 **Massage your memory.** Use every memory technique you've learned to maximize what you're able to retain and recall.

- 💡 **Know when to surrender.** When you can't remember your name or stay focused, give up and get some sleep.

- 💡 **Consider an early-morning rather than a late-night cram**, especially if you're a "morning" person. I've found it more effective to go to bed and get up early rather than go to bed late and wake up exhausted.

💡 **When you arrive at the test site**, spend the first few minutes writing down whatever you remember and are afraid you will forget, such as formulas, equations, dates, and so on.

Speaking of tests, please turn to Chapter 12 for your final exam.

Look How Much You've Learned!

Test 1: Random numbers

Here is a much longer number than the one in the initial quiz you took before reading this book. How many digits (of 50) can you memorize in five minutes?

23940729626121410710521410729142084312133495971400

Test 2: Random words

Now there are 50 words. Does your memory palace have enough space for all of them?

Drawing	Raw	Football
Water	Acrobat	Saxophone
Cart	Sandbox	Pansy
Elbow	Magazine	Licorice
Brave	Adding machine	Pancetta
Symbol	Supermodel	Essay
Territory	Duct tape	Escargot
Ascot	Smartphone	Derrick
Bear	Green	Pipe
Prancing	Midget	Refrigerator
Deluge	Javelin	Cheetah
Kitty	Uniform	Ocean
Bank	Blacksmith	File folder
Forage	Ace of clubs	Broom
Stamp	Ferrari	Lawn chair
Discuss	Missle	Dalmatian
Etching	Diamond	

Test 3: Less-familiar English words

Here are 25 English words that are obscure or, at least, less familiar. How many can you remember (with definitions, of course) in five minutes?

Denudate	To make bare, strip
Celature	The art of embossing metal
Harmotome	A zeolite mineral that occurs in twinned crystals
Mesocarp	The fleshy part of certain fruits
Anthema	An eruption of the skin
Quaternary	Consisting of four
Baccate	Berrylike
Parotic	Situated at or near the ear
Waddy	A cowboy
Frisket	A mask of thin paper laid over an illustration
Yaud	An old, worn out mare
Golliwogg	A grotesque person
Peristyle	A colonnade surrounding a building or open space
Rerebrace	A piece of armor for the upper arm
Echinate	Bristly, prickly
Neo-Dada	A minor art movement of the 1960s

Millime	An aluminum coin of Tunisia
Impartible	Indivisible
Clamant	Noisy
Blepharitis	Inflammation of the eyelids
Cochlea	A spiral-shaped cavity in the inner ear
Vexillum	A military standard carried by ancient Roman troops
Ramify	To divide or spread out into branches
Oleiferous	Giving rise to oil
Crandall	A tool for dressing stone

Test 4: Names

Can you remember these 15 international dog breeds and their primary countries? Spelling counts!

Bully kutta	Pakistan
Rajapalayam	India
Vizsla	Hungary
Gran Mastin Borinquen	Puerto Rico
Mucuchies	Venezuela
Wetterhoun	Netherlands
Broholmer	Denmark
Alpine Dachsbracke	Austria
Telomian	Malaysia
Schipperke	Belgium

Sapsali	Korea
Kur	New Zealand
Tosa	Japan
Akbash	Turkey
Samoyed	Siberia

Test 5: Foreign vocabulary

Let's visit Paris and learn some French!

Seiche	cuttlefish
Demain	tomorrow
Colombe	dove
Haricot	beans
Joie	glee
Timbres	stamps
Piège	trap
Jaune	yellow
Étang	pond
Bar	sea bass
Grillon	cricket
Maintenant	now
Éclair	lightning
Jeudi	Thursday
Jumeaux	twins

Doué	gifted
Dinde	turkey
Champignon	mushroom
Parrain	godfather
Chaussettes	socks

Test 6: Dates and events

Can you recall all of the pertinent names, dates, and events after studying the following list for five minutes?

Aspirin was invented in 1899 in Germany by Dr. Felix Hoffman.

John Adams and Thomas Jefferson died on the same day (July 4, 1826).

The Treaty of Versailles, which ended World War I, was signed in 1919.

In 1896, the U.S. Supreme Court case *Plessy v. Fergusen* ruled that "separate but equal" was a constitutional philosophy for the treatment of different races.

February 18th is Pluto Day, the anniversary of its discovery in 1930.

Theodore Geisel (Dr. Seuss) was born in Springfield, Massachusetts, in 1904.

The modern Olympic Games were first held in Athens, Greece, in 1896.

The FBI's "10 Most Wanted Fugitives" program began in March 1950.

The American Medical Association was established in 1847.

On March 4, 1917, Jeanette Rankin became the first elected woman to take a seat in the U.S. House of Representatives.

Dmitri Donskoi defeated the Tartars in 1380 and became the Grand Duke of Moscow.

William Howard Taft arrived in the Philippines in 1901 to become its first U.S. governor.

Pearl Buck won both the Noble Prize in Literature (1938) and the Pulitzer Prize (1931).

The British surrendered Singapore to the Japanese on February 15, 1942.

The ambulance was created for Napoleon's Army in 1792.

The Sacagawea golden dollar (which contains no gold) was introduced in January of 2000, replacing the Susan B. Anthony dollar, which had been in circulation since 1979.

Francis Hawkins wrote a manners book for children in 1641—when he was 8 years old.

The Tokyo-Osaka bullet train, which reached a top speed of 130 mph, made its first run in 1964.

Test 7: Reading

Can you read the following passages and write a brief summary? Will you remember the pertinent facts and figures tomorrow?

The World Population

Odds are you'll never meet any of the estimated 247 human beings who were born in the past minute. In a population of 6 billion, 247 is a demographic hiccup. In the minute before last, however, there were another 247. In the minutes to come there will be another, then another, then another. By next year at this time, all those minutes will have produced 130 million newcomers to the great human mosh pit. Even after subtracting the deaths each year, the world population is still the equivalent of adding one new Germany.

The last time humanity celebrated a new century there were 1.6 billion people here for the party—or a quarter as many as this time. In 1900 the average life expectancy was, in some places, as low as 23 years; now it's 65, meaning the extra billions are staying around longer and demanding more from the planet.

But things may not be as bleak as they seem. In country after country, birthrates are easing, and the population growth rate is falling.

Cheering as the population reports are becoming today, for much of the past 50 years, demographers were bearers of mostly bad tidings. It was not until the century was nearly two-thirds over that scientists and governments finally bestirred themselves to do something about it. The first great brake on population growth came in the 1960s, with the development of the birth-control pill. In 1969 the United Nations created the U.N. Population Fund, a global organization dedicated to bringing family-planning techniques to women who would not otherwise have them.

Such efforts have paid off in a big way. According to U.N. head counters, the average number of children produced per couple in the developing world—a figure that reached 4.9 earlier this century—has plunged to just 2.7.

But bringing down birthrates loses some of its effectiveness as mortality rates also fall. When people live longer, populations grow not just bigger but also older and frailer.

For now the answer may be to tough things out for a while, waiting for the billions of people born during the great population boom to live out their long life, while at the same time continuing to reduce birthrates further so that things don't get thrown out of kilter again.

According to three scenarios published by the U.N., the global population in the year 2050 will be somewhere between 7.3 billion and 10.7 billion, depending on how fast the fertility rate falls. The difference between the high scenario and the low scenario? Just one child per couple.

The Invention of the Sewing Machine

Prior to the Industrial Revolution—that period of rapid industrial growth that began in England in the mid-18th century and then spread to other countries over the next 150 years—there really wasn't a pressing need for a sewing *machine*. *People* were the sewing machines. In a time when cotton was harvested by hand, wool was shorn by hand, and leather was handcured, handcut, and handstitched, the making of clothing was slow-paced. It was usually done on a small scale by the women in the family, and usually only for their own family's use. Tailor shops served to fulfill whatever other needs a society had, but they were individual enterprises in which every item was a handcrafted, one-of-a-kind creation.

The Industrial Revolution launched the era of mass production, and introduced manufacturing processes that have never ceased to expand and improve. One of the major advancements was in the area of fabric production. Suddenly, cotton was picked and cleaned by machine, mills rolled out great bolts of material; companies sprang up to produce and sell garments and other items made from fabrics, such as towels, tablecloths, and curtains. Seemingly overnight, hand-sewing everything became impossible.

Early versions of sewing machines were created in England and France, but they were completely unworkable as commercial machines. Thomas Saint's machine, for example, designed in 1790 to sew leather, was never even built. Barthelmy Thimonnier invented a machine in France in the late 1820s that sewed a chain stitch using a crocheting needle. He enjoyed some success with the machine sewing soldier's uniforms for the French Army, but his shop and machines were destroyed by rampaging tailors who believed that Thimonnier was set on putting them out of business and that any machines designed to replace human labor were sinful.

Walter Hunt, the inventor of the safety pin, was the first American to invent a sewing machine. In 1832, he built a machine that worked, but it had its problems. It could only sew a straight seam, the work could not be manipulated or turned under the needle, and the seam's maximum length was only a few inches.

In 1838, Hunt tried to convince his daughter to start a corset manufacturing business using his machine, but she refused, believing, as did the French, that machines that replaced humans were immoral. Hunt never patented his machine.

A few years later, Elias Howe, then working as an apprentice in a machine shop, decided to try his hand at designing and building a sewing machine; specifically a machine that could mechanically duplicate the individual motions of his wife when she was sewing by hand. After several false starts and dead ends (often unknowingly precisely duplicating Walter Hunt's trials and errors), Howe built a machine that could sew a seam. In the summer of 1845, he demonstrated the machine to a clothing manufacturer in Boston and, with his machine, sewed five seams by himself faster than five girls did working on only one each. The manufacturers were impressed, but they didn't buy any machines from Howe.

Howe went to England with a new partner, but was bamboozled by his new investor and left alone in London with no job and no money. He ultimately returned to America, where he was amazed to find that his machine had become quite popular, but that his original partner had sold the patent without compensating him. After a series of contentious court trials, Howe was awarded his patent and began earning thousands of dollars a year from sales of his sewing machine. He ultimately died a rich man.

How did Isaac Singer figure into this potpourri of deception, confusion, and bitterness? Singer was part of a team of sewing machine manufacturers who the court ruled had to pay Howe royalties for his invention. Singer had invented his own machine in 1851, but his invention used a foot pedal instead of a hand crank. Nonetheless, soon after he patented his machine, he ended up being sued by Howe for patent infringement. As we know, the court ruled in Howe's favor. Although, in all fairness, it is a historical fact that essentially the same sewing machine was invented independently by three men: Walter Hunt, Elias Howe, and Isaac Singer.

As to who was the ultimate winner, have you seen any Howe or Hunt sewing machines in the stores lately?

In case you were wondering

The long number in quiz 1 can be transformed into a single sentence: "Numbers can be changed into words quite easily and words can be transformed into memorable pictures, yes?"

Appendix

Suggested Peg Words for Numbers 21 to 100

21	Nut, wand, knight
22	Nun, noon, onion
23	Name, enemy, gnome
24	Nero, wiener, whiner
25	Nail, kneel, gnarl
26	Notch, wench, hinge
27	Nag, neck, wink
28	Knife, knave, nova
29	Nap, knob, nip

30	Mouse, moose, mass
31	Meat, mud, mouth
32	Moon, man, money
33	Mom, mummy, mime
34	Mayor, mower, hammer
35	Mail, mole, mall
36	Match, mush, image
37	Mug, mike, hammock
38	Muff, movie
39	Map, mop, imp
40	Race, horse, ears
41	Radio, rose, art
42	Rain, horn, urn
43	Room, worm, arm
44	Rower, rear, warrior
45	Roll, rail, rule
46	Roach, rash, arch
47	Rock, rug, ark
48	Roof, reef, wharf
49	Rope, harp, ruby
50	Lace, walls, lice
51	Light, lid, lead
52	Lion, loon, lawn
53	Loom, lamb, elm
54	Lyre, lure, lawyer

55	Lily
56	Leech, ledge, latch
57	Log, lake, elk
58	Leaf, loaf, wolf
59	Lip, elbow, lip
60	Chess, juice, shoes
61	Chute, jet, shed
62	Chain, gin, ocean
63	Chime, jam, gem
64	Chair, jar, shower
65	Chili, jail, shawl
66	Judge, choo-choo
67	Chalk, jug, sheik
68	Chef, java, chief
69	Chip, jeep, ship
70	Case, goose, kiss
71	Cat, goat, kite
72	Cane, gun, queen
73	Comb, gum, gym
74	Car, gear, crow
75	Coal, glue, quail
76	Cage, couch, cash
77	Cake, gag, keg
78	Calf, cave, coffee
79	Cap, cube, cup

80	Face, fuzz, vase
81	Feet, photo, food
82	Fan, phone, vine
83	Foam, fame
84	Fire, fur, ivory
85	Fly, veil, flea
86	Fish, fudge, effigy
87	Fig, fog
88	Fife
89	Fob, fib, fop
90	Bus, pies, pizza
91	Boat, pot, bed
92	Bone, pen, piano
93	Bomb, poem, bum
94	Beer, pear, boar
95	Bowl, pill, bell
96	Peach, beach, bush
97	Book, pig, puck
98	Beef, pave, puff
99	Baby, pipe, papa
100	Daisies, disease, diocese

Index